So, You Want to Buy Your First House

A Step-By-Step Guide to the Do's
and
Don'ts of Buying Your First Home

Tracy McKnight

Dedication

This book is dedicated to my dad. He is the reason for my perseverance. He has taught us all what a work ethic really means. I remember him telling me more than once, "You can do it."

Acknowledgment

There are a number of people that need to be credited for this book.

My best friend in the world, my love, Daphne Casses, is the person who encouraged me to start writing. Her support has been unwavering throughout this process.

To Joshua, Jessica, Patrick, Amanda, Ashley, Zack, Claudia, Aubrie, Madix, Landon, Logan, and Lillie, I can not wait to see what each of you become.

To Terry, Teresa, Mom, and Dad, in my mind, you are the definition of what a family truly is.

About the Author

Tracy McKnight lives in Gladewater, Texas, where he takes care of his family. He enjoys traveling, concerts, reading, watching a great movie, and, of course, selling real estate!

He still works every weekday selling real estate and believes in the notion, *"If I'm not talking to people about real estate, I'm not making any money."*

Preface

This book is an attempt by Tracy to highlight the advantages that first homeowners have and how it can become a way to not only create wealth but also a stable future. In this book, you will find examples of how people have made their fortunes and achieved goals through real estate that have helped them succeed in life. While doing so, Tracy also guides readers on how they can easily traverse through the often tricky and relatively long journey of buying a home.

If you have ever had a dream home or wanted to purchase your first property, then this book is for you. Even if it is not your first go at real estate, the tips and guidelines provided within these chapters will help property enthusiasts avoid making mistakes that can cost a fortune and ensure a smooth home-buying process. Another interesting bit in the book is an emphasis on reliance upon official data and certified professionals, such as those from relevant property associations such as the National Association of Realtors (NAR).

Combined with Tracy's guidance and experience, the data insights will allow you to understand the home-buying process and be prepared for any hurdles or mishaps. With this book, you will be covered every step of the way, and you will not have to go through a significant loss or a bittersweet relationship with your realtor, homebuying agent, or lender. The book aims to equip you with enough information and guidance that you make informed and planned steps that lead you to be happy in a home that you can love and live in!

Contents

Chapter 1: Why Home Ownership is Important

I have lived in East Texas all my life, and Gladewater is where I live and work as a real estate broker. My parents attended Gladewater High School in the early '50s, where they saw performers like Elvis Presley and Johnny Cash. My father had several convenience stores back when I was a kid in the '70s, '80s, and '90s. I grew up working in our stores, and that is where I learned how to deal with people of all kinds.

My Journey

When I initially started to gain some experience and interest in real estate, I worked in construction as a day laborer. My father helped me secure a job pouring concrete. During this time, I lost over 100 pounds that first year, and I took a break from college, too.

The experience allowed me to gain the motivation I required to finish college and get my degree. I think my father did all that by design! He is tricky like that, but I really appreciate his wisdom and foresight! After that, I received my Bachelor of Science degree in 1992 from the University of Texas in Tyler.

During college, I saw my older brother and sister finish their college education and become gainfully employed. My sister worked as an accountant for a large service company. Meanwhile, my brother was a special education teacher, and his wife was a speech therapist at the school. They both worked as teachers for over 30 years!

This also inspired me to understand the importance of teaching and how it can allow us to polish ourselves as well as serve others. In pursuit of this spirit, I received a Texas Teacher's certificate that I hold to this date. It was my brother who suggested I get a teacher's certificate.

After I invested some time in the construction business, I eventually decided to take my interest to the next level, and I received a real estate license as a realtor in 1996. This is when I realized the importance of home ownership and how valuable it is. The complications and multi-organizational processes of securing a mortgage were what made me realize that people were struggling with all of these things.

So, I felt like I needed to do something about it to add value to my clients as I worked on mortgages and cleared deals. As I gradually made my way up and helped clients, I ended up with insurance licenses in the State of Texas for the following sectors: health, home, and auto insurance. I could then sell my customers home owners insurance to go with their new home.

My family has been a great influence on my life. I thought that I would be working at the secondary level in a high school here in Texas. Instead, I opted to teach in a prison for almost 20 years! To say that I have a great appreciation for teachers is an understatement.

Teaching inmates was a truly humbling and learning experience. It made me realize how lucky I was to have parents of the kind that I did and the teachers who truly cared about my future. Working in the prison is the core reason that I became so interested and inclined toward real estate. My schedule was such that I would begin teaching at five in the morning, and I would end just after lunch. I had the entire afternoon to pursue something else as a way to make a little extra money to provide for my family.

Having to speak before a group of, at times, hostile strangers proved to be great for me, and I credit my poise to teaching. If you ever want to learn something, then I suggest that you approach it with the intent that you must teach it to others as well — especially those who are incarcerated since they are very tough on any teacher.

Just like middle school and high school students, those guys would know if I was unsure about something. It was like a shark sensing blood in the water. I made sure that I always had a plan and a backup as well before every class.

The classes that I would teach were not 45 minutes long. No, I was scheduled to teach the same guys for three hours. But in hindsight, it was quite a fun and exciting journey, too. For most of my career, while teaching in prison, I taught a GED class.

We would spend most of the time practicing math and how to write a simple essay. The result was that I had close to 2,000 successful GED graduates from my classes over the course of my career. And it is not just that I only taught them, but I also learned a great deal about people that would help me in real estate sales.

I worked as a realtor in the afternoons when my classes were over. After I received my broker's license in 2008, Dad and I bought our little office. Within five years, the building was paid off, and we were dealing not only with new customers but also customers who had traded at Dad's stores. Six years later, I quit the prison and started selling full-time, working for the *"Me Company,"* as I like to call it.

Dad taught me many important things; perhaps one of the most important was this. He said, *"It's not necessarily what you know but who you know."*

When I stopped to think about it, I realized he was right. Every job I have ever had was through someone I knew. The opportunities that I have had were from people known to me.

After working as a teacher, I also realized that I like to help other people. And I discovered I could do a lot just by listening to their problems.

The Benefits

So, now that you know my journey, let's get straight back to the point of this book: how to own your own home. I will help you understand what processes and stages will come along. This is what will distinguish you as a successful and confident homeowner.

Wealth Creation

Homeownership is often seen as a pathway to building wealth, and rightly so. Here, I will explain a bit about how owning a home compares to renting and why it's a wise financial choice. One of the most compelling aspects of home ownership is the opportunity to build equity. Equity is essentially the part of the home you own outright, and it grows as you pay down your mortgage. Consider it a forced savings plan.

In fact, David Bach, a renowned financial expert and author, emphasizes the "Latte Factor" — the idea that small daily expenses can add up to the cost of a mortgage payment. This can clearly help you understand how you can redirect your spending and contribute it towards home ownership. The way to trim your budget is simple: If it is not necessary to spend the money, don't.

I will illustrate the financial benefits of this equity growth over the years through personal experiences, emphasizing that it is an investment in your future. Owning a home provides a level of stability that renting cannot match. It allows you to put down roots, establish a sense of belonging in your community, and provide control over your living space.

In a fast-paced world, this stability is invaluable, especially for families. So, how do you build wealth with a home? Let us take a look at an example:

The average home's value appreciates currently at the rate of about five percent a year. After renting for a year, what does the renter have, but only a decreased checking account? Yes, you are sheltered, and the landlord does take care of the maintenance, repairs, and insurance, but besides that, you receive very little value for your money.

And by the way, the landlord's insurance often only covers the residence, not your belongings. For that, you will need a renter's insurance. So, God forbid if the house you are renting burns down and you don't have a renters' insurance policy!

When you own your home, every time you make a payment to the mortgage holder, several things happen. First and most important, a part of each payment goes toward paying back the principal or money you borrowed to purchase the home. And in return, you get an equal amount of equity.

The rest of the payment goes toward property taxes and interest on the loan. In fact, most of the first payment is interest, and very little goes toward the principle. Consider a 30-year $335,000 loan at 5.27%. When the loan is paid off, you will have paid more in interest than the total you borrowed. But you are building equity, and the value of the home does appreciate each year.

A simple example of equity is if you owe $75,000 on your home and it is worth $100,000 now, you may not realize it like most people, though this means that you have $25,000 in equity! Speaking of equity, here are a few examples of how home ownership can build wealth. Similarly, in 1971, my family bought a brick home on a slab, a 3/2 — or about 1600 square feet — for $25,000. Today, that home is worth $190,000, according to the county records, whereas the actual market value would probably be closer to $220,000. Similarly, the home I bought in 2002 for $102,000 is now worth about $250,000.

Other than this, it is common knowledge that the real estate market has historically shown that property values tend to appreciate over time. This is referred to as 'home appreciation.' By examining trends and experiences, I will help paint a picture of how your home's value can increase, adding to your net worth, as we proceed in this book.

Your home essentially becomes an investment that grows in value as you build memories within it. Knowing about the housing market, its history, and future predictions also plays an important role in how and where you purchase a home. You should always consult experts and incorporate analysis of qualified real estate professionals before deciding on which house to purchase.

How do you learn about the market in your area? Go to any realtor's office and ask for a spreadsheet of recent sales in your area. Most realtors will welcome the chance to get to know a new potential seller or buyer. You could do this weekly in the months leading up to the time you expect to purchase a home.

The future of the housing market plays a vital role in building your wealth. It could help you understand the potential for appreciation and growth in the coming years, multiplying your wealth over time and providing your future generations with a solid base to start.

Understanding the Wealth Building Aspect

We will delve into the historical trends and expert opinions, highlighting how homeowners can benefit from this appreciation. Recent housing market data on home price appreciation in Texas and the United States can shed light on the matter.

Professionals use the Case-Shiller Home Price Index or the National Association of Realtors (NAR) to gain official data since it is both reliable and technical. They also provide insights to highlight current trends, and this helps reflect (or rather show) the potential for wealth accumulation. I will be using these two sources throughout the book. Then, when it comes to understanding wealth-building, you can use data and analyses from home ownership and realtor associations, as well as some of the research centers, to gain valuable insights into how home ownership affects different demographic groups in different areas.

Elaborating on the Benefits of Homeownership

So, you can clearly see that building wealth and financial growth are benefits a home can lead you to. But you should also know that it can lead to other benefits. The benefits of owning a home, emphasizing its contribution to financial security and personal well-being, are tremendous as time goes on.

Tax Benefits

Homeownership comes with a range of tax advantages. These include deductions for mortgage interest and property taxes, which can put more money back in your pocket. It is like an added reward to the financial benefits of owning a home. Next is the sense of security and relief that comes with knowing that you have a home and can do anything that you want in it — unlike in a rented home.

Freedom and Personalization

Often, renting comes with limitations on how you can personalize your living space. In contrast, owning a home offers the freedom to make it truly yours. You can paint the walls, renovate the kitchen, or build that dream backyard. Your space reflects your personality and preferences, adding to the quality of life that home ownership brings. Also, you become part of a select group that owns a home, and it is reflective of your struggle and the rewards that came along your journey.

Other Benefits of Home Ownership

If you have children or are planning on having any, you can benefit them by owning your home. According to a study from the Joint Center for Housing Studies of Harvard University (by Donald R. Haurin, Toby L. Parcel, and R. Jean Haurin), the children of homeowners experience a higher quality of home life and have higher scores in school than the children of those who rent.

Success Story

Did you ever notice how, on some job applications, there is a question about whether you own or rent? Have you ever wondered why? There is a simple reason for that, and it is one that people overlook.

To employers, owning a home is a sign of stability. Homeowners are much less likely to leave for another opportunity because they are invested in the property. Sure, renters are, too, to some extent. Renters will likely stay if they must pay to get out of a lease. But that is much less stressful compared to if you have to suddenly sell your house before leaving. Also, some leases are month-to-month, meaning the tenant can choose to stay or leave at the end of each month's rental term. You might wonder, '*But I have never bought any real estate, so what can I do now?*'

I would tell you to relax first! Real estate sales go on every day of the week. Well, at least the title companies and lenders don't work on the weekends, but the realtors do. They do — trust me! There are agents out there showing land, homes, and commercial properties every day of the week! In fact, contracts are even signed in the middle of the night, in-person or online! That fear factor can be dealt with by finding an experienced agent. We will discuss how to find a great agent later.

Overcoming Hurdles to Homeownership

Despite the numerous benefits, buying a home can be a daunting prospect. Many times, a first-time home buyer will call and ask to see a home on the market. An experienced agent will ask if the buyer has been pre-qualified for a home loan.

If the buyer has never asked about their credit score, they probably have little chance of getting a loan. So, check your credit now. Go to annualcreditreport.com and request your free credit report. You can sign up for free annual credit reports while you are there.

When you receive your report, look for errors, which you have the right to challenge. Write a letter to the reporting credit bureau detailing the error and include copies of any documents pertaining to it. Keep copies of everything you send.

Disputes with credit bureaus can take 30 days or more, and the credit bureau must respond to your dispute, whether it justifies an increase to your score or not. For an FHA loan, your score must be at least a 500 with a 10% downpayment or a 520 with a 3.5% downpayment. An easy way to raise your score is to borrow a little money from your banker. Save $100 and see your banker. Tell the banker you want to borrow $100 and use the $100 you saved as collateral. When the bank loans the money to you, don't spend it. Save it until the note matures and pay the loan off.

It will cost you a little interest, but the bank will report that you paid the note on time, and it will improve your credit. Borrow $200 next using the same process. You can do this multiple times to raise your score.

If you have a score of at least 600, then see a mortgage broker now. As you will see, there are programs to help first-time home buyers.

Affordability: The myth that homeownership is financially out of reach for many can deter aspiring buyers. I will break down this myth and discuss various financial options and assistance programs available, making homeownership more accessible in the coming chapters.

Maintenance and Responsibilities: The idea of home maintenance can be intimidating. I will provide valuable tips on managing maintenance and responsibilities effectively, helping homeowners maintain the value and comfort of their homes.

Market Volatility: Housing market fluctuations can create uncertainty. Consider the 2008 financial bubble burst that was due to predatory housing loans made by unscrupulous lenders who only cared to make the loan and then sell the note to another lender. Also, low supply can drive market volatility and foster bidding wars. Sentiment can cause a seller or a buyer to place too much value on a property. Appraisers use cold, hard facts to value a property. All of these things come together to create volatility in the housing market. You must remember a property is only worth what someone, a capable someone, will pay for it. Generally, residential property and raw land will appreciate a small percentage every year. Commercial property is a tale for another book.

This brings us to the types of loans that are at the disposal of first-time home buyers, veterans, and the rest of the lot. I would like you to understand some basics pertaining to FHA, USDA, and VA loans. These are the terms that you might have heard of but not know much about.

Understanding FHA, USDA, and VA Loans

Specialized loan programs are ideal for first-time home buyers and can help unlock financial opportunities that they were previously unaware of.

The loans that we are about to discuss are designed to facilitate home ownership and cater to specific needs.

So, let us get down to it and explain a bit about these loans and what we will discuss in the coming chapters.

FHA: It is an abbreviation for Federal Housing Administration, which provides a type of loan guarantee. FHA loans are a fantastic option, especially for first-time home buyers. Congress created the Federal Housing Authority in 1934 during the Great Depression. It grew out of a time when only one family in 10 owned a home and 9 out of 10 rented.

Getting a regular conventional home loan then required a 50% down payment and repayment of the balance in 3 to 5 years. Needless to say, during the depression, very few had 50% for a down payment.

FHA does not make loans; it guarantees loans. It protects the lender that does make the loan. If the buyer defaults on the loan, the FHA pays a claim to the lender for the unpaid balance. The object of an FHA loan is to make it easier to own a home and protect the lender.

Typically, an FHA loan also has a lower rate. These loans have lower down payment requirements and are accessible to those with credit challenges.

Often, an FHA loan will require a 3% or better down payment. There is a way to roll that down payment into the loan itself. An example of that is a $200,000 offer made for a $200,000 home using an FHA loan.

The buyer needs $6,000 or 3% for a down payment. The price of the house on the contract can be bumped up to $206,000, and the seller will have to concede that extra $6,000 back to the buyer at closing to be used as a down payment. The seller still gets what the seller wanted, $200,000, and the buyer gets to use the $6,000 for the down payment.

The only caution is at the house must be appraised for $206,000. If a home does not appraise at or above the contract price, the contract must be renegotiated.

USDA: The United States Department of Agriculture, in full, also guarantees loans. USDA loans are designed to support home ownership in rural and suburban areas. I will discuss the unique aspects of USDA loans, its eligibility criteria, and the benefit of zero down payments for qualified buyers.

These are popular in small rural towns with a population of less than 20,000 as these are the only areas eligible for USDA loans.

VA: Veterans Affairs or VA loans serve veterans and active-duty military personnel in achieving home ownership. I will explore the advantages of VA loans, their eligibility requirements, and the unique benefits that they offer, including the possibility of a zero down payment.

To get a VA loan, you must be an active service member, veteran, or qualifying surviving spouse with a certificate of eligibility. VA loans require no down payment but must only apply to primary residence and must meet lender requirements. There is no home inspection required. An appraisal is required. There is no limit on the amount of the loan as long as the borrower is qualified.

Conclusion

There are realtors who specialize in selling homes to FHA, USDA, and VA borrowers. They are very familiar with the processes and which lender is the most efficient for making these particular loans. If this is your choice, call the local real estate office and ask for such a realtor.

Home ownership is a journey that encompasses financial growth, stability, and the fulfillment of the American dream. In this chapter, we've explored why home ownership is significant for building wealth and security, detailed its numerous advantages, addressed common concerns, and provided a thorough understanding of FHA, USDA, and VA loans.

Chapter 2: Navigating The Credit Report

The dream of owning a home is now well within your reach, but there are crucial steps and financial insights you need to consider. In this chapter, we will delve into the depths of the home-buying process and explore the intricate world of credit.

In order to obtain a good deal on your home loan, you need to understand a bit about what constitutes a credit report and how to review it.

You do not want to be stuck paying for a 20- or 30-year mortgage on terms that could have been easier if you had tried an expert's opinion.

In doing so, I will not only elaborate on the things to look out for in a report but also provide tips that will aid you in managing your debt and improving your credit score and credit history. So, let us begin and inform you on how you can make it successfully through the process!

The Home Buying Process

A simple way to determine how much house you can afford is the following. Usually, a house payment, including interest and property taxes, is about 1% of the amount borrowed. So, for example, if you wanted to buy a $220,000 home in today's market, your payment would be about $2,200 a month. If your monthly rent is $ 2,200 now, then you are probably good to go forward. To be sure, you need the help of a professional. Take a copy of your budget and see a lender.

The NAR emphasizes the importance of starting your home-buying journey with a pre-approval for a mortgage.[1] I want you to understand why this process is important.

This step not only helps you understand your budget but also demonstrates to sellers that you're a serious buyer. So, if you would like any offer made to be credibly viewed, then I suggest that you consider pre-approval as the first stage.

Next, you should ideally find and collaborate with a realtor who can suggest real estate that can fall in line with your credit profile and budget. At the same time, you would also consider their expertise as they would know more about the locality and its issues than anyone.

Similarly, the Consumer Financial Protection Bureau (CFPB) also advises homebuyers to consider not only the purchase price but also factors like

---

[1] Synovus, Helpful Mortgage Info For Your Buyers National Realtors Association. February 7, 2022.
https://www.nar.realtor/magazine/real-estate-news/sales-marketing/helpful-mortgage-info-for-your-buyers

property taxes and insurance when setting a budget. They offer useful online tools to help you calculate these costs. See the website at consumerfinance.gov

Since the pre-approval process is worse than having your qualifications vetted for a job, the step is recommended by NAR. While it is not a simple process to undertake, certain documents are required, such as:

- **Proof of Income:** W-2 forms, pay stubs, bank statements, and any other proof of income may be required. This information is necessary in order for banks and specialists to determine if you can afford the mortgage.

- **Tax Returns:** Given that essential information about your wealth and income is revealed in the tax returns, lenders put considerable importance on this document.

- **Debts:** Next up, any lender would need to know how much debt you owe as a mortgage applicant.

Ideally, a 10 or 20 percent ratio is good. In certain scenarios, a lender may rely on this ratio even more than a credit score. It can be most appropriate in case someone is a relatively new borrower or one with a first home ownership loan.

- **Assets:** Any investments, savings accounts, bonds, or other assets that you hold enhance the buyer's financial profile. This can provide security against your loan. Putting up extra collateral can help you gain a good deal.

- **Residence history:** Past addresses, including landlord references, may be required. This reflects upon your character and provides assurance about your profile as well as your payment history.

- **Documentation of any down payment assistance:** If the buyer is utilizing down payment assistance, it could take longer to process the mortgage due to third parties. In fact, FHA and conventional lenders forbid the use of borrowed money for a down payment. If you're lucky enough to have family that wants to help you get into a house, any money they want to give you for a down payment must be in your account for at least 60 days prior.

Enter the Home Buying Process

Given the things involved, as you can see, buying a home is a monumental decision. It requires careful planning and thorough understanding.

Assess Your Financial Health:

Before you embark on this journey, it's essential to evaluate your financial situation. This involves understanding your income, expenses, and overall financial stability. Take time to calculate your debt-to-income ratio, which helps you determine how much house you can afford. The debt-to-income ratio sounds like complicated math to some, but it is a simple comparison of how much money you make each month to how much you are obligated to spend each month on regular bills.

Build and Review Your Credit:

Your credit score plays a significant role in securing a mortgage with favorable terms. Later in this chapter, we will explore the steps to obtain and manage your credit report.

1.   **Set a Budget:** Determine how much you can comfortably spend on a home. Consider not just the purchase price but also other expenses like property taxes, maintenance, and insurance. Consider how much you are paying for rent now. That figure is probably, barring any unforeseen monetary windfall you may suddenly have, what you can afford monthly.

Most people who are living day to day hate to look at their own finances because it reminds them of their current situation. Diligent attention to a budget shows where you can save for that down payment and get out of the rent cage. Review your finances at least weekly.

2.   **Pre-Approval for a Mortgage:** As explained at the start of this section, this step is highly recommended as the first one by NAR. Get pre-

approved for a mortgage from a reputable lender. This step gives you a clear idea of the loan amount you're eligible for, which helps when shopping for homes. I know I am starting to sound like a broken record, but this is really important.

3. **Find the Right Real Estate Agent:** A knowledgeable and trustworthy real estate agent can be your guide throughout the home-buying process. They help you find suitable properties, negotiate offers, and handle paperwork. Remember to ask a potential realtor what they have sold recently. A good realtor stays busy.

4. **House Hunting:** Explore properties in your chosen location, keeping in mind your budget, needs, and preferences. It's important to be patient in this phase; finding the perfect home takes time.

5. **Make an Offer and Negotiate:** Once you've found the home you desire, work with your real estate agent to make an offer. Expect negotiations between you and the seller before arriving at a mutually acceptable price. If you are going to sell something on the open market, how would you price it? Like most people, 99% at least, you will ask a little more than what you truly want in order to give room to negotiate. The next question you ask yourself is how much of a discount I would take, 5%, 10%, or 20%? Putting yourself in the shoes of others will help a great deal when negotiating.

6.   **Inspections and Appraisals:** After your offer is accepted, inspections and appraisals are conducted to ensure the home is in good condition and that the sale price is reasonable. A home inspection is good for your peace of mind. An appraisal is for your lender's peace of mind.

7.   **Secure Financing:** Finalize your mortgage application and secure the loan. Pay close attention to the interest rate and loan terms. Your lender will tell you once you are finally approved. Most of the time, you will have a "lock" on your interest rate that is only good for so many days. If the deal is extended, you could lose your rate lock and have to begin applying all over. Stay in touch with your lender. A good lender will tell you if time is short.

8.   **Closing:** The final step involves signing documents, paying closing costs, and officially becoming a homeowner. Most buyers have the impression that everyone, buyers, sellers, lenders, and agents, will be at the closing at the same time. That does not happen all the time. In fact, I would prefer that the parties close separately. You never know what one will say to the other.

Now that you have an overview of the home-buying process, let's shift our focus to credit.

Understanding Your Credit Report and Profile

Your credit report is a detailed history of your credit usage and payment behavior. It's essential to obtain and regularly review your credit report for accuracy and completeness. Here's how you can obtain and assess your credit report:

Obtaining Your Credit Report:

1. AnnualCreditReport.com: This website is the official platform for obtaining a free credit report from each of the three major credit bureaus (Equifax, Experian, and TransUnion) annually. Visit this site and follow the simple steps to request your report.

2. Credit Monitoring Services: Many financial institutions offer credit monitoring services that provide regular access to your credit reports and scores. Some of these services are free, while others may require a subscription. You probably have a credit card now that offers a free look at one of your credit scores. Have you looked at it?

Reviewing Your Credit Report

1. **Check for Accuracy:** Review each section of your credit report carefully. Verify that your personal information, accounts, balances, and payment history are accurate. Any inaccuracies could negatively impact your credit score.

2.   **Look for Negative Items:** Pay attention to any negative information, such as late payments, collections, or public records. Identify discrepancies and potential errors.

3.   **Dispute Discrepancies:** If you find inaccuracies, you have the right to dispute them. Each credit bureau has a dispute process. Follow their guidelines to challenge and correct any incorrect information.

Improving Your Credit Score

A strong credit score is crucial when applying for a mortgage. It can significantly impact your interest rate and loan terms.

The following are some quick, intelligent, and informed tips to boost your credit score:

1.   **Manage Your Debt:** Keep your credit card balances low. High credit card utilization can negatively affect your score. Aim to use less than a third of your available credit.

Hint: If you pay the full balance each month, no interest will be charged.

2.   **Pay Bills on Time:** Consistently pay your bills by the due date. Payment history is a critical factor in your credit score. Consider setting your utility payments to auto-payment mode or bank giro as it is known in Europe. You will sleep better knowing you

don't have to worry about whether you paid your power bill. These auto payments will also go toward a better credit score.

3. **Avoid Opening New Credit:** Each time you apply for credit, it triggers a hard inquiry, which can slightly lower your score. Minimize new credit applications, especially when you're in the process of buying a home. Better still, don't borrow any money when you are looking to buy a home!

4. **Diversify Your Credit:** A mix of different types of credit (credit cards, installment loans, mortgages) can positively impact your credit score—however, only open new accounts when necessary.

5. **Keep Old Accounts Open:** The length of your credit history matters. Keep your oldest accounts open to demonstrate a longer track record of responsible credit use.

6. **Regularly Monitor Your Credit:** Use credit monitoring services or annual credit reports to stay informed about your credit status. This helps you catch potential issues early.

7. **Seek Professional Help if Needed:** If your credit issues are more complex, consider consulting a credit counselor or financial advisor for guidance.

So, what is a credit profile, and how does it differentiate from a credit report, you may wonder? Equifax explains that your credit profile is an assessment of your creditworthiness. They go on to say that it is comprised of a credit score and credit report, which are generated using data from your credit history. Your credit profile can help credit providers determine whether you qualify for a credit card, loan, or service and on what terms.

According to FICO, the credit profile is a detailed summary of an individual's past and present credit history as reported to the credit reporting agency by lenders who have extended credit to you. These lenders have the right to report your loans, credit, and payment history to any or all of the three major credit reporting institutions: Equifax, Experian, and TransUnion.

A credit report, on the other hand, is a document that provides detailed information about your credit history that is prepared by a credit bureau. It includes information such as your personal information (name, current and previous addresses, social security number, and employment history, etc.), details on your credit accounts (credit cards, loans, etc.), your payment history, and any negative marks on your credit, such as missed payments, public records such as bankruptcies, and a list of entities that have asked to view your credit report.

Credit reports also list credit inquiries and details of accounts turned over to credit agencies, such as information about liens and wage garnishments.

Generally, credit reports retain negative information for seven years, while some bankruptcy filings typically stay on credit reports for about ten years.

Credit reports are important because they are used by lenders, landlords, and other financial institutions to assess your creditworthiness. They use the information in your credit report to determine whether or not to approve you for credit, and it is also used to determine the terms of that credit, such as interest rates, fees, and sometimes the term length of the credit.

So, how do you obtain your credit report? Fortunately, you are entitled to one free credit report from each of the three major credit reporting agencies (Equifax, Experian, and TransUnion) every year. You can request your reports from each agency separately, or you can get all three at once from AnnualCreditReport.com.

Once you have your credit report, it's important to know how to read and interpret it. Here are some things to look for:

Personal Information

Make sure that all of the personal information on your report is correct. This includes your name, address, and social security number. Make certain that there is only one name, your current address, and your correct social security number appears on your credit report.

Credit Accounts: Look at your credit accounts to see if they are all accurate and up-to-date. Check to see if the balances and payment history are correct.

Credit Inquiries: Check to see if there are any inquiries on your report that you don't recognize. Inquiries can lower your credit score, so it's essential to make sure they are all legitimate.

Negative Marks: Look for any negative marks on your credit report, such as missed payments or collections. These can have a significant impact on your credit score, so it's important to address them as soon as possible.

Dispute Errors: If you find errors or inaccuracies on your credit report, you have the right to dispute them with the credit reporting agency. Disputing errors can help improve your credit score and ensure that your credit report is accurate.

Credit reports are an essential tool for understanding your overall credit health. By obtaining your credit reports, reviewing them regularly, and disputing errors, you can ensure that your credit report is accurate and drastically improve your creditworthiness over time.

It's also important to understand how credit reporting agencies collect and use information. Credit reporting agencies gather information from a variety of sources, including lenders, landlords, and public records. Additionally, you provide information to the credit reporting agencies when you apply for credit. They use this information to create your credit report, which lenders and other institutions then use to assess your creditworthiness.

One thing to watch out for is identity theft. Identity theft occurs when someone uses your personal information (such as your name, social security number, or credit card number) to open accounts or make purchases without your knowledge. If you notice any unfamiliar accounts or charges on your credit report, it's important to take immediate action to protect yourself.

In addition to reviewing your credit report regularly, there are other steps you can take to protect your credit. One of the most important things you can do is monitor your credit report. You can do this for free using a variety of tools and services, including credit monitoring services and free credit score websites.

Another way to protect your credit is to be vigilant about your personal information. This includes protecting your social security number and other personal information, as well as being careful about sharing personal information online.

Incorporating these strategies into your financial habits can lead to a healthier credit score, which, in turn, can pave the way for more favorable mortgage terms and contribute to your long-term financial well-being.

As you venture into the journey of buying a home, remember that both the home-buying process and your credit health are interconnected. A thoughtful, informed approach to both aspects will empower you on your path to homeownership and wealth generation. Stay committed to your financial goals, and you'll find yourself unlocking the doors to your dream home sooner than you think.

Credit Score

Now that you have explored the home-buying process and what constitutes a credit report, you need to understand how all of it is related to your credit report and credit score. A credit score is crucial because it influences the terms of the offer presented by the lender, including whether the loan is approved or denied.

Your score will ultimately determine the loan amount, interest rate, fees, and other terms that are placed on the loan or credit. An individual with a credit score lower than 670 is considered a subprime borrower — basically, a risky and problematic borrower.

Such a score automatically indicates to financial institutions that their approval of loans for subprime borrowers should ideally involve charging substantially higher interest rates compared to those with a good score. The higher cost for this loan to subprime borrowers is to accommodate for the risk of loaning money to someone with a higher tendency of defaulting.

There may also be a shorter time frame for them to pay back the loan as well. In the same vein, someone with a higher credit score — preferably above 760 — stands a better chance of getting better deals than a subprime borrower. This is simply because the credit score makes the borrower appear more appealing to lending institutions and poses fewer risks to them.

This implies that he would be given a longer time to pay up and a lesser interest rate as well. So, the next question that may pop into your mind would be how to improve your credit score, and I will guide you on the matter.

Improving Your Credit Score

Before I tell you how to improve your score and what forms part of it, I would like to provide you with some professional advice and recommendations that are common throughout the industry.

The National Association of Mortgage Brokers (NAMB) advises potential homebuyers to focus on paying down high-interest debts before applying for a mortgage. This can improve your credit score and increase your chances of securing a favorable loan.

Experian, a leading credit bureau, recommends a strategic approach to credit improvement. They advise setting specific goals for your credit, such as reducing credit card balances and tracking your progress over time.

MyFICO, which is a division of the industry-leading credit-score organization FICO (Fair and Issacson Company), suggests that keeping credit card balances below 10% of your available credit limit can have a substantial positive impact on your credit score.

The three major credit bureaus — Equifax, Experian, and TransUnion — all recommend that you obtain your credit report from AnnualCreditReport.com.

They stress the importance of checking all three reports because discrepancies may exist between them. Credit counseling agencies, such as the National Foundation for Credit Counseling (NFCC), recommend an annual review of your credit report to spot and dispute errors promptly.

FICO, the company behind the widely used FICO credit scores, suggests that paying bills on time is one of the most effective ways to boost your credit score. They emphasize the significance of maintaining a consistent payment history.

Remember the simple way to improve your credit score that was discussed earlier.

Summing Up

In conclusion, credit reports are an important tool for understanding your credit history and financial health. By obtaining your credit reports, reviewing them regularly, and taking steps to protect your credit, you can improve your creditworthiness over time and protect yourself from identity theft and other forms of financial fraud. The information in your credit report, therefore, is the primary source to generate credit scores.

FICO further points out that your credit report lists what types of credit you use, the length of time your accounts have been open, and whether you've paid your bills on time. It tells lenders how much credit you've used and whether you're seeking new sources of credit. It gives lenders a broader view of your credit history than other data sources, such as a bank's customer data.

Incorporating these insights and suggestions can aid you in your home buying and credit management journey and can significantly enhance your prospects. These collaborative insights are designed to help you make informed decisions, secure a good deal, and avoid pitfalls that could hinder your path to home ownership and wealth generation.

Remember, the journey to home ownership is a process that requires careful planning and financial diligence. Armed with the knowledge and expertise shared here, you are better prepared to navigate the intricacies of the home-buying process and master your credit, ultimately realizing your dream of owning a home. Stay committed to your goals, and success will be within your reach.

Chapter 3: Finding Professionals to Help

By now, you must have realized how important it is for you to be cautious and prepared for the home-buying journey. Finding the right professionals to guide you is what you should do next.

According to the National Association of Realtors (NAR) 2013 report on the profile of buyers and sellers in real estate, a staggering 92% of the people revealed that they began their quest to buy a home via the Internet. This is the arena where qualified professionals and industry leaders have captured the market, and it is an easy place to begin your journey. However, I will try to provide you with additional and deeper insights from the industry!

With my experience in the real estate industry, I will help you navigate through the hurdles and avoid any mistakes that people generally make. Just because someone is on the internet does not mean that what they say is true and that it applies to your case, too! Clearly, the local expert's experience and knowledge play a vital role in your learning more about the area and real estate.

While all of this may be overwhelming, you should remember that buying your first home is an exciting yet complex journey, so this is why you need to do it thoughtfully and positively. It is essential to have the right professionals by your side to help you navigate the process. This chapter will emphasize the value of seeking assistance from local professionals during the home-buying journey and provide strategies for finding and evaluating real estate agents, lenders, and other related professionals. Additionally, you will come across a list of important questions to ask when selecting a realtor or lender to ensure a good fit.

The Value of Local Professionals

Like any industry, real estate is also localized, as discussed in the last chapter. The thing about it is that given its nature, what works in one area may not necessarily apply to another. This is where local professionals and specialized experts come in. Along your journey, you will come across a variety of people, from licensed agents or registered realtors to qualified lenders and brokers, and they are the ones who can make your estate dream come true. This is because they possess invaluable knowledge of the local market. There are some key reasons for which they are vital.

They are as follows:

Local Market Expertise

It's quite self-explanatory, but the local professionals have a deep understanding of the neighborhood dynamics, property values, and market trends. Local knowledge is invaluable in real estate. A skilled agent knows which neighborhoods are up-and-coming, which have good schools, and which fit your lifestyle. They can spot a good deal a mile away.

They can basically guide you to the right neighborhoods that match your preferences and budget. One of the first things that you need to understand is that leading brokers recommend scheduling interviews with several agents to understand their approach, experience, and communication style.

This is because the leading brokers and local professionals have established relationships with other key players, such as property inspectors, appraisers, and contractors. This network can make the process smoother and more efficient, as they can recommend trusted service providers.

Whenever you are interacting with these experts, you should always keep an open mind and ask questions about the neighborhoods that you may be interested, recent market trends, and their experience in the area. A well-informed agent can guide you effectively and tell you about the key things that distinguish an area as well as what makes it stand apart from others.

According to the National Association of Realtors (NAR), nearly three-forth of home-buyers believe that a real estate agent's local knowledge is critical in their home search. This is why people go for experienced realtors because these professionals have a deep understanding of the local neighborhood dynamics, property values, and market trends.

Networking

Relying on a network of professionals is crucial since they help you along every step of the way. Using the network, you not only gain local knowledge but also gain access to other professionals and data that is otherwise inaccessible. For instance, you might get to know that someone is selling a home for a dirt cheap price because they need to get the money quickly.

While this is just a small example, it goes on to show how much your network can play an important role in acquiring your dream home for the right place. As cited earlier in the book, according to the NAR, almost nine in ten home-buyers purchased their home through a registered real estate agent (Realtor) or broker in 2021. This underscores the pivotal role that agents play in the home-buying process.

Legal and Regulatory Knowledge

Once you are done with the creation of a local network and basic knowledge, you need to learn to understand the process, as explained in the previous chapter. But by this time, you will know the basics and will need to get into the nitty-gritty. The legal and regulatory knowledge is often ignored since it is left to professionals, but you should read up on it, too. At the very least, you should discuss these things with the professionals.

One thing that you need to understand is that real estate transactions involve a lot of legal and regulatory complexities, from estate, valuations, and mortgage paperwork to real estate association by-laws and local state regulations (especially taxes). All of these things need to be considered and known before you finalize an area or type of home that you would like to acquire.

Your network will play a vital role here since the local professionals are well-versed in local laws and can ensure that your home-buying-related transactions comply with all the necessary regulations. And this brings us to perhaps the most underrated yet crucial aspect of the home-buying process —negotiation.

Having said that, real estate transactions go on every day. Should you have any legal questions at any time, then seek an attorney for answers.

Negotiation

While you should be prepared for most of the things since it will allow you to make informed decisions in the real-estate journey, negotiation is something that should often be left to the professionals. Seasoned real estate agents and lenders excel in negotiation, helping you secure the best deal possible.

According to the NAR, real estate agents' negotiation skills are highly valued. They can help you secure the best deal possible, whether you're buying or selling a property. In 2021, a quarter of the home-buyers reported that negotiating the terms of a sale was the most challenging aspect of the home-buying process.

Here are some things to remember about negotiating. First, most sellers will ask for a price that will give them room to haggle. Just so you know, most of the time, the asking price is just that, an asking price. And most sellers know they probably won't get the asking price. Second, once an offer is made and declined, the next party to speak loses.

As in this example, a seller has rejected a $90,000 offer on a property with an asking price of $100,000. If the buyer wants it, the buyer will then make a counter offer of more money or offer to pay additional closing costs for the seller, something to sweeten the deal. If the buyer hesitates when making this counter, the buyer may learn something about the seller. The seller may not want to lose a capable buyer and contact the buyer's agent before the buyer makes a counter. The buyer then knows the seller is willing to compromise more. Many times, parties will make a counter and wait for the other to speak first. When that happens, one knows the speaking party is willing to concede more.

The negotiation stage can also be used in the process with your lender and mortgage expert. The Consumer Financial Protection Bureau has found that nearly half of home-buyers do not shop around for a mortgage. This is a significant gap, as preparing for a mortgage can save buyers money on the payment plan, the installments, and interest rates.

The study also revealed that getting a single additional quote can save $1,500 on average while getting five quotes can save $3,000. Lastly, choosing the right lender is as important as finding the right home. The lender you work with can impact your long-term financial health. Don't be afraid to pit one lender against another. For example, if one offers a 6% rate and the next one offers 6.5%, tell the second lender you already have a 6% offer. Give that lender a chance to beat it. The lender might do it just to get your business.

So, look out for lenders who offer transparency, competitive rates, and responsive communication.

Let me try to give you an overview of the things that you need to do to evaluate them.

Finding and Evaluating Real Estate Agents

One of the best ways that you can start with is through word-of-mouth.

Personal recommendations, especially from trustworthy resources, are essential if you are looking for reliable professionals. So, you can easily start off by asking your friends, family, or colleagues for recommendations. They may have had positive experiences with local agents.

Honestly, in this case, even negative experiences will allow you to learn from your mistakes and avoid choosing the wrong people. After all, you do not go around buying houses every now and then. This is why remaining aware, (relatively) knowledgeable, and cautious has been stressed throughout the book.

Personal Recommendations

In fact, let me tell you that recommendations are still one of the most trusted ways to find a reliable real estate agent. That's how most business is done in the world, and the real estate industry is no exception. Next, it is not necessary to have references available from the people closest to you.

If you come across someone who is reliable, you can also request references from their previous clients and follow up with them to gauge their performance and experience. Real feedback and follow-up will prove to be extremely valuable.

Research

Next up, one of the easiest things that you can do is review the professionals and experts on their websites and social media profiles. These days, every professional wants to have their presence online so they can increase their chances of securing a good deal or client.

One of the key things that you need to do is look for professional qualifications such as REALTOR®, which indicate a commitment to ethical standards. Also, always ensure the real estate agent is licensed and a member of the National Association of Realtors (NAR). This signifies adherence to a code of ethics. It's a mark of professionalism and commitment.

Interview Multiple Agents

Lastly, when you have finally made up your mind, you should always try to be sure. The leading brokers recommend scheduling interviews with several agents to understand their approach, experience, and communication style. This can help you determine who aligns best with your goals.

It is not the end of the line, and you should always ask questions. Do not hesitate to ask anything if it does not make sense or if you are confused since you should remember that it is a matter of you spending a significant chunk of your lifetime wealth and savings. So, do it wisely and slowly, and you will do fine.

Evaluating Real Estate Professionals and Lenders

Having understood what you need to do, you should understand that once you shop around, you will be able to clear your confusion. Once you have cleared the professional, check their credentials to be sure. Call the relevant association or agency that they are associated with to ensure that the expert is licensed and accredited. Dig up online for reviews and ratings.

When it comes to lenders, you should always be curious about loan programs or ongoing first-time home-buyer schemes. These are often quite reasonable, and they might prove to be of help to you financially! When you enquire about the various programs being offered, you will be able to find one that best suits your needs.

At this stage, you will be able to contact multiple people, such as lenders, to get quotes and compare interest rates, fees, and terms.

Questions to Ask When Selecting a Realtor or Lender

For Realtors

1. How long have you been working in this area, and what neighborhoods do you specialize in?

2. Can you provide references from past clients who were first-time homebuyers?

3. How do you plan to communicate with me throughout the home-buying process?

4. What is your approach to negotiation, and can you share success stories from previous deals?

5. What have you sold recently?

For Lenders

1. What types of mortgage loans do you offer, and which do you recommend for a first-time buyer like me?

2. What are the current interest rates, and can you explain how they might change throughout the loan process?

3. What fees and closing costs can I expect to pay, and are there any programs or incentives available to me?

4. What is the timeline for loan approval and closing, and how do you ensure a smooth process?

5. Can you provide an estimate of the total monthly mortgage payment, including taxes and insurance, for a home in my budget? Lenders are required to give you a "good faith estimate" that provides how much your monthly payment is, what your rate will probably be, closing costs, and other details.

In conclusion, partnering with the right professionals is crucial for a successful home-buying journey. Local experts bring invaluable knowledge and guidance, making the process more manageable and ensuring you make well-informed decisions.

Creating a network can be crucial in your home-buying journey, and it will allow you to not only find the right people but eventually come up with the right deal for your dream home.

By following the strategies and asking the important questions outlined in this chapter, you'll be well on your way to finding the perfect real estate agent and lender and helping yourself achieve your homeownership goals.

Chapter 4: Location, Location, Location

The three most important factors when buying a home are location, location, and location. Too often, I hear people talking about making decisions based on the home itself instead of the location, and that is a mistake. So, what is it about the location that makes it so vital to real estate investing?

One of the reasons why location is so important in real estate is that buyers often want and need close access to amenities and transportation options. This means relative proximity to restaurants, grocery stores, dry cleaners, shopping, and entertainment venues. It could also mean a home situated near essential roads and public transportation options, such as bus stops, subway stations, and public bike-share locations.

When looking at a home, be sure to assess how close it is to these important amenities. Unless you're looking to buy a vacation home on an almost deserted island, proximity to amenities will typically improve a home's value. I will help you unveil the heart of the home-buying process.

Let us further explore the significance of location and what factors are to be considered when finalizing your real estate options.

Why Location Reigns Supreme

The age-old saying that echoes the significance of location in real estate is often encapsulated in the mantra: '*location, location, location.*' This is not just a cliché, but rather, it is a fundamental truth. Most buyers out there primarily assess their potential property, a house or apartment, that they intend to purchase by looking at the underlying crucial factor — the plot of land on which it stands.

Whether nestled in the heart of suburban tranquility or within the bustling streets of a city, the geographical positioning of a property defines its intrinsic value. The irreplaceable nature of the location, unaltered by renovations or remodeling, drives the essence of a home's worth.

The Lure of Location

Embracing the ideal location becomes a strategic investment choice. Urban blocks, akin to the essence of a neighborhood in the suburbs, can be categorized by people as 'good' or 'bad,' and these things exert a significant influence on property values. But let me tell you that it is not as simple as that.

The principle is clear: the intersection of supply and demand. Real estate within coveted locations is limited, which fuels their demand and derives their ultimate value. There are a few factors that allow value to be placed, and it should be considered before making a final decision.

The truth of the matter is that all neighborhoods are changing, and so are their dynamics in the medium-to-long run. Thus, the evolving nature of neighborhoods cannot be understated. It should be noted that today's less desirable locality might blossom into the 'next big thing,' or a rather good area, within a couple of years.

Factors such as the influx of major employers, infrastructure developments, or upcoming commercial expansions can pivot a once-forgotten area into a coveted location. There are also certain factors that need to be considered when scouting for your ideal abode.

Thus, take into account the following five pivotal elements:

The Five Factors

1. **Centrality:** Your chosen city or town impacts the housing cost, with highly developed cities like San Francisco commanding premium prices. The outskirts often bear the brunt of population shifts, impacting property values.

2. **Neighborhood Dynamics:** Accessibility, aesthetics, and essential amenities contribute to a neighborhood's allure. From efficient transportation

routes to the desirability of community spaces, these factors shape a neighborhood's appeal.

3. Future Development: Future-oriented and long-term buyers consider not only the present facilities but also future infrastructural upgrades. Therefore, planned developments in education, healthcare, and public transit play a crucial role in enhancing property values.

4. Lot Location: The placement of a house within a neighborhood matters, too. Proximity to busy roads or commercial areas can affect pricing. Conversely, properties offering scenic views or waterfront locations hold greater value.

5. The Home and Lot Dilemma: In a quandary between a pristine house on a small lot versus a fixer-upper with a generous expanse, prioritize the lot. Houses can undergo renovations, but the immutable value of a well-located lot prevails.

The future value of the property is largely based on the five factors that we discussed, but other things need to be considered in the research as well. Hence, you should also keep the following things in mind that can allow you to foresee if the location is truly good enough or not.

Predicting the Future: Location Foretelling Value

Neighborhoods shift, and locations transform. It has a significant impact on the value. Therefore, understanding the pulse of a community, observing shifts in trends, and recognizing the potential of an area to evolve can guide and transform you into a shrewd buyer.

After all, you need your investment to be rewarding enough in the future. You should always remember that today's "undesirable" locale might harbor tomorrow's real estate gem.

So, what are the other things that you need to keep in mind, you may ask?

The Millennial Influence

As the largest cohort in the home-buying landscape, millennials are reshaping the real estate market. Their preferences favor budget-friendly homes with stellar schools and accessibility to amenities—driving the demand that, in turn, elevates property values. So, if you would like to settle down for good or keep a value in the long run, then settle where the millennials are moving.

Not only will the housing market be relatively affordable, but the school district and economic opportunity will be better than in other areas. The potential is vastly immense in an area where millennials are moving into. This brings us to the point as to how you can distinguish between one neighborhood from another.

Unveiling Neighborhood Potential

What delineates a sound neighborhood investment? The scope stretches beyond the present. Envisioning future developments, contemplating school district expansions, and assessing planned civic enhancements underscore the intrinsic value of a neighborhood. There are also a few basic things that should be considered, such as follows:

Community Vibe: Evaluate the local community to understand if it aligns with your lifestyle. Some may prefer a bustling city center, while others may seek a quiet suburban setting. Assess the neighborhood's culture, diversity, and social activities.

Safety and Crime Rates: Prioritize safety; research crime rates in the area to ensure you are moving into a secure environment. Neighborhood safety is a fundamental concern for any potential homeowner.

Research by academic institutions such as the University of Pennsylvania or studies published in journals like "Housing Studies" reveal the correlation between safety and property values. Generally, areas with lower crime rates tend to have higher property values.

> Accessibility to these amenities not only ensures convenience but often determines the desirability and value of a location.

Local Government and Development Plans — Property Values and Potential Appreciation

Examine historical property values in the area. Understanding how property values have fluctuated over time provides insights into potential future appreciation. Factors like gentrification, upcoming developments, or local government initiatives can impact property values.

Zoning and Development: Investigate local government plans, zoning regulations, and proposed developments. Understanding the future landscape of the neighborhood can provide clues about the potential direction of property values.

School Districts: For families or future resale value, the quality of school districts is pivotal. For this reason, research school ratings and their impact on the community.

Embracing Local Amenities

Local amenities aren't mere conveniences; they're value generators. The presence of essential facilities—grocery stores, dining, and entertainment options—within a short reach reinforces the allure and price tag of a neighborhood.

Research the proximity of essential services like schools, hospitals, grocery stores, public transportation, and recreational facilities. Accessibility to these amenities not only ensures convenience but often determines the desirability and value of a location.

Online Tools and Community Engagement

Online Resources: Leverage online tools like real estate websites like Zillow, Redfin, and Realtor.com, neighborhood guides like City-data.com, and forums to get a comprehensive understanding of the area.

Community Engagement: Engage with locals, visit the neighborhood at different times of the day, attend community events, and talk to potential neighbors. This immersion helps in understanding the community dynamics and your potential satisfaction with the area.

The Transport Conundrum

An aspect often overlooked is the ease of commute. The proximity to transportation hubs, be it highways or public transit, garners higher desirability and concomitant property appreciation.

Studies by real estate research institutions like Zillow or Redfin highlight the impact of amenities on property values. Proximity to public transportation, schools, parks, and shopping centers can significantly influence property prices.

The Enduring Impact of Location

The unique charm of a location profoundly influences property values. The innate supply and demand dynamic, intertwined with the desirability of an area, orchestrates the steady appreciation of real estate.

The significance of location in the home-buying decision cannot be downplayed. The location impacts lifestyle, convenience, and future property value. It defines your daily routine, accessibility to amenities, the quality of the neighborhood, and even the potential appreciation of your investment.

Property Valuation and Comparables

Comparative Market Analysis (CMA) is something that experts utilize in the industry. CMA reports compare similar properties in an area. This comparison provides an estimate of a property's value based on recent sales of comparable properties.

Real estate agencies and market research firms often release local market reports, highlighting neighborhood-specific data, average property values, and trends. Leveraging these reports offers a detailed understanding of micro-level market dynamics.

Barbara Corcoran, real estate mogul and investor, stresses the critical role of location in property values. She emphasizes that the location of a property is one of the primary factors influencing its future appreciation.

Another resource that you should consider is the Federal Reserve Economic Data (FRED), which provides access to various economic indicators like employment rates, GDP growth, and mortgage rates. Analyzing these indicators assists in understanding the broader economic climate and its impact on property values.

Reports from real estate analytics firms like CoreLogic or ATTOM Data Solutions offer insights into housing market trends, foreclosure rates, and market stability, aiding in making informed decisions about property values.

So naturally, you should seek professional appraisal reports for a detailed assessment of a property's worth. This detailed evaluation helps in determining a property's reasonable value. Certain factors contribute to the value of the property in these reports, and I will help highlight some of them.

Economic Indicators and Housing Market Data

According to the National Bureau of Economic Research, there is a definite correlation between school expenditures and home values in any given neighborhood. A report titled, *'Using Market Valuation to Assess Public School Spending,'* found that *"for every dollar spent on public schools in a community, home values increased $20."*

These findings indicate that additional school expenditures may benefit everyone in the community, whether or not those residents actually have children in the local public school system.[2]

Lastly, there are a few pieces of advice that the National Association of Realtors suggests people know, such as the following:[3]

- *"Homes in school districts sell more quickly than those in lower-quality school districts.*

- *They typically hold their value more than those in lower quality ones.*

---

[2] How Your Property Value is Affected by a Nearby School District, UpNest, Jan. 22, 2021)
https://www.upnest.com/1/post/property-value-affected-by-school-district/
[3] Schools & the Homebuying Decision (nar. realtor)
https://www.nar.realtor/schools-the-homebuying-decision

- *They command higher selling prices than those in lower quality ones."*

Perhaps this is why Robert Shiller, a Nobel laureate economist, underlines the significance of understanding market data and economic indicators in making informed real estate decisions. He advocates for analyzing long-term trends to decipher potential future property values.

By integrating these industry insights, expert opinions, and credible data sources, the book not only provides a comprehensive understanding but also offers a well-rounded perspective on the pivotal role of location, the intricacies of neighborhood evaluation, and the interpretation of market data in the context of home-buying decisions.

Conclusion

Having understood the importance of location and the elements that lead to the value of a property, we can understand that the crux of the home-buying experience hinges on the critical decision — location over the house. Therefore, you should opt for the potential of a locality over the house's current state.

The unchanging allure of a location remains the quintessence of a wise real estate investment. The exploration of location is not merely a page in the book of home-buying; it's the preface to a thriving investment and an enriched living experience.

This chapter delivered a comprehensive understanding of the pivotal role of location in the home-buying journey, catering to the needs and aspirations of diverse homebuyers.

In the next chapter, we will elaborate upon the factors that play a crucial role in determining what property is best for you. This will include the longer-term things and other things to consider before you decide which property you would like to call home.

Chapter 5: Determining What Type of Property is Best for You

So far, we have discussed the importance of buying your dream home and identified steps that you can take to find the home that fits your requirements and dreams. Once the location and objective for the property are clear, the budget is the first thing you will need to work on if you want to find your home.

Therefore, there is a need to blend your emotions with financial decisions before you finalize the budget and ascertain the type of home that suits you the most. To navigate this journey successfully, understanding your budget and maintenance capacity is paramount, just as location and finding the right people are important.

For individuals entering the real estate market for the first time, acquiring knowledge and conducting thorough research are essential. Don't rush into a decision based solely on the property's appearance or price tag. You will still need to consider the location, amenities, resale value, and potential growth of the neighborhood.

If you look at some of the data from Realtor.com, you will see that it indicates that properties in neighborhoods with good schools tend to have higher resale values, making them a smart investment choice. So remember the following as a rule when you are trying to ascertain your budget:

"First-time buyers should focus on long-term value rather than immediate savings. Considering factors like location, resale potential, and neighborhood growth is essential for a sound investment."

This is where a professional will become truly helpful to you. You should enlist the guidance of a reliable real estate agent who understands your budget constraints and helps explore suitable options. They can provide valuable insights and help you navigate the complexities of property types, guiding you toward a choice aligned with your financial capabilities and lifestyle.

The Mortgage Bankers Association reports that enlisting the expertise of a real estate agent can potentially save buyers up to 5-10% on the purchase price! Remember that finding an ideal home isn't just about meeting your present needs; it's about securing a place that fits your future aspirations while being financially sustainable. Let us delve into why this matters and how to make informed choices.

Recognizing your financial capabilities and maintenance capacities is crucial during the homebuying process, as a well-maintained house tends to incur lower maintenance costs. Now, envision the alternative scenario if you hadn't made these plans. I will delve into an in-depth discussion of the fundamental aspects that have been previously highlighted.

You should also ensure that you know how to set a budget and keep contingencies in place for repairs and maintenance. Then, I will explain some home options that can be considered to bring out more value for your money.

Before you start falling in love with that charming cottage or that sleek apartment, you need to take a step back and assess your financial situation realistically.

Understanding Your Budget and Maintenance Capacity

You need to determine your budget by considering your income, savings, debts, and other ongoing expenses. You will eventually find out how much money you can save and how you can allocate towards mortgage payments. Similarly, you need to be aware that allocating a portion for a downpayment, closing costs, and emergency funds are the key features of any real estate deal that need to be kept in mind.

Additionally, it's essential to emphasize that your financial obligation doesn't conclude with the closing process. When it comes to possessing any lasting, tangible asset, be it a vehicle or property, a significant aspect involves ongoing maintenance and potential repairs. In the real estate industry, acknowledging the necessity of continuous maintenance and addressing unforeseen repairs is of utmost importance.

A survey conducted by the National Association of Home Builders showed that renovation costs for distressed properties can surpass initial estimates by 20-30%. This is why setting aside a maintenance budget becomes crucial. Yet, at the same time, it is equally important that you choose the right type of home and one of decent build quality, too.

The budget for maintenance and repairs should typically be around one to three percent annually of your home's value. This will help you mitigate and manage any unanticipated expenses. But note that you need to be cautious so as not to stretch your budget to its limit during the purchase phase.

In a study conducted by the Consumer Financial Protection Bureau, cited by Financial Deposit Insurance Corporation (FCID), 28% of homeowners encountered unexpected expenses during the first year of homeownership.[4] This finding emphasizes the necessity of budgeting for unforeseen costs.

---

[4] https://www.fdic.gov/analysis/cfr/consumer/2022/presentations/low-presentation.pdf

Homeownership requires financial planning beyond the initial purchase.

You also need this peace because many homes are foreclosed due to a lack of planning by homebuyers, which leads them to miss out on payments. On average, every year, around 6% of Americans face difficulty paying back the installments and managing the payment schedules.

On top of it, external factors, such as inflation and increases in interest rates, can also hamper your ability to manage and keep a hold on your payments. This is essentially why the 20-30% of debt to income ratio is recommended, so you have ample to save and leave a margin to spend.

Allocating funds for maintenance, therefore, not only protects your investment but also offers you much-needed peace of mind during unfortunate situations. Next up, you will need to leave a little room for crucial ongoing costs, such as essential renovations and changes that suit your requirements and allow your home to provide you with the comfort you need.

Different Property Types and Considerations

So, let us explore what type of housing options are available to homebuyers. These vary as each type caters to the diverse needs and preferences of different people. From conventional houses to condominiums, townhouses, and even Housing and Urban Development repossessed properties (HUD repos), each has its pros and cons.

First-time buyers might find HUD repos to appear quite appealing due to their potentially lower prices. However, it's vital to approach these properties with a hint of caution. While they offer affordability, they might require extensive repairs or renovations, potentially surpassing your initial budget.

Keep in mind that such improvement costs should not exceed a fifth of your property's value, as stated by the National Association of Home Builders survey. A market analysis by Zillow indicates that HUD repos can be priced significantly lower than the market value, up to 20-40% less, making them attractive for budget-conscious buyers.

HUD repos, as per data from the Department of Housing and Urban Development, can be an excellent option for buyers willing to invest time and resources in renovations, potentially yielding a higher return on investment. Similarly, you will need to consider the fact that possessing a HUD repo is not directly available to buyers.

There is an entire process in which HUD-recognized realtors and agents can only partake in a bidding process. The bids proceed 30 days after a property has been foreclosed, and 5-6% commissions have to be paid. So, you should keep these things clear when opting for HUD as your first-time property.

Next up, you should know that HUD can allow you to withdraw up to $10,000 from your 401(K) or other pension schemes if you are a first-time buyer. Given that this is a federal government rule, if your spouse also has not bought a home before, then the two of you can get access to $20,000 for the purpose of expenditure for your first home.

You will need to be cautious, though, since spending the money is essential in order to be eligible for the 10% penalty waiver that is not available to people who prematurely withdraw from their pension schemes. The amount taken as part of the first-buyer withdrawal from pension needs to be allocated and spent within 30 days. Otherwise, you will have to be ready for the 10% penalty on the value of the withdrawals.

Being aware of such considerations will provide you with a clear understanding of renovation costs and their crucial role before you decide to dive into HUD repo purchases.

Hud repos are not for beginners. In order to reap the benefits, a buyer must be familiar with contracting any lender-required repairs or be certified to do it themselves. A buyer may not know all the issues present in a HUD repo until the work begins and may need much more liquid funds to correct it.

Next up, condominiums appeal the most to buyers seeking homeownership without the full maintenance responsibilities. However, for those eyeing HUD repos, conducting a thorough cost-benefit analysis considering renovation expenses is crucial.

Condominiums are quite a common choice for Americans, and 27% of the country's population live in these developments. The reason for this is simple: they cost less than a house, and the buildings, as well as the common areas surrounding the premises, are maintained by Housing Associations (HOAs).

While this seems to be a reasonable choice, the problem is that HOAs have their own membership fees and bureaucratic procedures that need to be considered before you decide to buy a condo.

A report by the U.S. Census Bureau indicates a rise in the popularity of condominiums among millennials due to their affordability and shared maintenance costs. In fact, half of all condominium projects built recently were constructed within the past 30 years.

So, the rising property prices might allow you only to have enough for a condo, but you will need to be aware of the pros and cons. A seasoned realtor and helpful attorney can help you understand your rights and benefits of buying a condo. A helpful estate agent can help you ascertain the true value, costs, and future market price for your investment.

By incorporating this guidance and insight in this chapter, you can strive to empower yourself to make informed decisions, guiding you towards a home that not only fits your budget but also complements your lifestyle and future aspirations.

Other Things to Consider

Before you finally make a decision, you should finally differentiate between your needs and wants. You should create a list distinguishing your non-negotiable needs. It will allow you to prioritize the location, number of bedrooms, and budget and compare it well with your wants, such as amenities — swimming pool, detached bath, fancy kitchen, garden, etc. This will help you prioritize essential features that you require and find your dream home.

The next thing that you will need to consider is future planning. You will need to envision your future needs based on your current needs. For instance, if you are a single professional, then it might seem logical to prioritize your home's proximity to your work. In contrast, you might need to consider that a growing family may mean you would need to focus on school districts and nearby amenities.

This is why you need to ask a lot of questions and ascertain what type of home would best suit your needs in the medium-to-long run. Ideally, a good investment will eventually pay off monetarily and mentally (through peace of mind and that of your family).

Lastly, if you still need clarification, then you should introduce yourself to worksheets where you can make a list of needs and wants to balance things that should be in your ideal home. Then, set out your budget and allocate the expenses accordingly to meet your home-payment targets.

If you weigh your lifestyle and desired amenities, then at least you will be able to figure out your budget and reach a conclusion about the type of home that would suit you the most. Next up, before you engage in and listen to expert opinions, ask your friends and family who have been homebuyers. Asking how they navigated the process might allow you to find the right balance.

At the very least, you will recognize the hidden knowledge of things to consider through their experience and highlight the things that should be kept in mind.

Understanding your lifestyle and envisioning your future needs is pivotal. It's not just about finding a house; it's about discovering a place that aligns with your life goals. In the next chapter, we will dive into the next step, which is to find someone to guide you.

In this case, it will be the right realtor who can listen to you rather than think about the cheque to guide you toward your dream home.

Chapter 6: How to Find a Realtor That Cares About You, Not Just a Paycheck

Anyone who has been a seasoned real estate professional with over ten years of experience will tell you that homebuyers often need to pay more attention to the importance of rapport with their realtor. For this reason, I need you to trust your instincts and choose someone who not only understands your needs but also makes you feel heard and valued.

This is the key because the person that you can get along and relate with will end up being the one whom you will probably trust.

You must have realized so far that the role of a professional will be crucial since at least one will be required to take you throughout the process — until you enter your dream home. So, in this way, it becomes important to note that your realtor is a key person, and the person guiding you will often need to be a seasoned and licensed professional.

Why You Need a Realtor for Your First Home Purchase

Purchasing a home is one of life's monumental decisions. Thus, your chosen agent should not merely offer a service; they should be a dedicated guide, a source of invaluable support, information, and expertise throughout this journey. Real estate agents go beyond mere transactions.

A reputable REALTOR® is meant to navigate you through the intricate process of buying a home. It's essential to choose an agent who isn't just reliable but also acts as a pillar of support, armed with insightful guidance.

Buying your first home is an exciting and rewarding experience, but it can also be daunting and stressful. You may be tempted to browse online listings and contact the agents who represent the properties you like, but there are better ways to find your dream home. In fact, you may end up wasting your time and money on homes that don't match your expectations or needs.

That's why you need a buyer's agent, a professional who works exclusively for you and your best interests. A buyer's agent is different from a seller's agent, who represents the seller and their property. The seller's agent pays a buyer's agent through a commission split, so you don't have to worry about any extra costs.

Remember the following three things while looking for a professional buyer's agent:

i)   Consult with real estate experts beyond your realtor. Home inspectors, appraisers, and contractors offer perspectives that aid in making informed decisions.

ii)   Stay informed about market trends, property values, and neighborhood dynamics. Online resources, real estate reports, and local market analyses provide critical insights.

iii) Optimize property viewings by preparing a list of questions and considerations beforehand. Take notes and pictures to aid in comparisons later. You can use some of the questions and tips that I have shared with you in the previous chapters.

A buyer's agent can offer you many benefits, such as enabling you access to listings, open houses, and information about where houses are about to sell. They would typically also know about some areas that they concentrate on, so they might have insights on the build quality, owner type, etc.

These things combine to play a huge role when you enter the negotiation and mortgage phases. The following are the things that you need to keep in mind when trying to ascertain and judge a helpful professional from an ordinary one:

- **Access to Listings and Information:** A buyer's agent has access to the Multiple Listing Service (MLS), which is a database of all the homes for sale in your area. They can also use their network and contacts to find homes that may not be advertised online or in the newspapers. A buyer's agent can also provide you with more details and insights about the properties, such as the history, condition, neighborhood, and market value.

- **Guidance and Advice**: A buyer's agent can help you narrow down your choices and find the best home for your budget, lifestyle, and preferences. They can also advise you on the current market trends, the best time to buy, and the best locations to invest in. A buyer's agent can also answer any questions you may have along the way and educate you on the home-buying process.

- **Negotiation and Representation**: A buyer's agent can negotiate the best price and terms for you based on their knowledge and experience. They can also handle the paperwork and legal aspects of the transaction, such as the offer, the contract, the inspection, the appraisal, and the closing. A buyer's agent can also protect you from any potential pitfalls or problems that may arise during the process, such as hidden defects, liens, or disputes.

- **Referrals and Resources**: A buyer's agent can connect you with other professionals and services that you may need for your home purchase, such as a mortgage lender, a home inspector, a lawyer, a title company, a moving company, or a handyman. A buyer's agent can also provide you with recommendations and reviews of these providers so you can choose the best ones for your needs.

A Lasting and Long-Term Relationship

So, given the many ways that a realtor and buying agent help you, you should note that since a buyer's agent is not just a one-time service provider, this is something that will go a long way.

If you consider the individual helping you into a long-term partner and resource, then you will opt for the right person and someone who does not only care for his paycheck. The reason for this is that even after you buy your home, you will still need to rely on your buyer's agent for any assistance or advice that you may need.

For instance, you may need to inquire about home maintenance, home insurance, home improvement, or even market analysis. Another important reason that a buyer's agent is crucial is so that they can help you sell your home in the future or help you find another home if you decide to move to another one.

This would mean that you would not need to restart this entire process of selecting a buyer's agent, and you would already have someone that you could rely upon.

So, how can you find a buyer's agent, where will it be possible, and how will it be fruitful enough for you to do so?

How to Find the Right Buyer's Agent

Finding a buyer's agent is easy enough if you know where to look and what to ask. Here are some tips to help you find the best buyer's agent for your first home purchase. Some of these tips have been referred to in the earlier chapters, but you will still need to consider these together and allow my input in this chapter to be judged and understood altogether.

- **Ask for referrals:** The best way to find a buyer's agent is to ask your friends, family, or colleagues who have bought a home recently for their recommendations. They can share their experiences and opinions with you and tell you why they liked or disliked their buyer's agent. You can also ask them for the contact information of their buyer's agent so you can reach out to them directly.

- **Do your research:** Before you contact or meet with a buyer's agent, do some background research on them. You can check their website, social media, online reviews, testimonials, and ratings to see their credentials, reputation, and track record. You can also look at their past and current listings to see the types of homes they specialize in and the areas they cover.

- **Interview them:** Once you have a shortlist of potential buyer's agents, you should interview them to see if they are a good fit for you. You can ask them questions such as the following:

  o   How long have you been a buyer's agent, and how many buyers have you helped?

  o   How do you communicate with your clients, and how often?

  o   How do you search for homes, and what tools do you use?

  o   How do you negotiate and handle the paperwork and legal issues?

  o   How do you deal with challenges or conflicts that may arise during the process?

  o   How do you charge for your services, and what are the costs involved?

  o   Can you provide me with references or testimonials from your previous clients?

Why Select the Best?

After you interview the buyer's agents, you should compare and evaluate them based on their answers, personality, and professionalism. You should choose the one who has the most experience, knowledge, and skills. At the same time, it should be someone who not only listens to you but also understands and caters to your needs. These are important things to note if you want the other person to understand your goals and match your style and expectations.

This is related to how connected the two of you feel and how easily you can communicate. The importance of this relatively minor aspect of selecting a homebuyer, but a pivotal role of the agent, has been underlined by the 2023 report on home buyers and sellers trend that has been published by the National Association of Realtors (NAR).

According to the NAR report, 83% of homebuyers consider a realtor's responsiveness a crucial factor in their decision-making process![5] This underlines the significance of finding a realtor who prioritizes effective communication and promptness.

Your homebuying agent has to be qualified and seasoned because he has many responsibilities to conduct, or at least have advanced knowledge of the following aspects to guide you most helpfully and comprehensively possible:

---

[5] National Association of Realtors Research Group, 2023 Home Buyers and Sellers Generational Trends Report, National Association of Realtors. 2023.
https://www.nar.realtor/sites/default/files/documents/2023-home-buyers-and-sellers-generational-trends-report-03-28-2023.pdf

- Conducting market research and analysis to assist in decision-making.

- Listing and strategically marketing properties for maximum exposure.

- Arranging and facilitating property showings and addressing queries from potential buyers.

- Expertly negotiating offers and counteroffers in your best interest.

- Coordinating inspections and appraisals to ensure property value.

- Serving as a liaison, ensuring seamless communication among all involved parties.

The Agent-Client Relationship is Important

The bond between you and your REALTOR® is crucial. It's an ongoing collaboration that necessitates trust, understanding, and mutual respect. Look for honesty, transparency, and a friendly disposition in your chosen professional.

You should also consider the following traits before you engage with and select a realtor and buying agent to help you in the homebuying journey:

Reputation and Track Record: Researching your agent's track record and reputation is vital. Browse through testimonials, agency ratings, and client feedback to gauge their credibility and reliability.

Communication and Reliability: Timely and effective communication is non-negotiable. Your agent should respect your time, acknowledge your preferred mode of communication, and promptly address your queries.

Expertise and Specializations: Consider agents with specific expertise matching your needs. Whether you're a first-time homebuyer or someone seeking new construction, finding an agent with relevant expertise can streamline your search.

Resourcefulness and Connections: An adept agent possesses the resourcefulness to navigate complexities and a network of trusted professionals. They should offer recommendations for lenders, inspectors, and other essential service providers.

In your quest for a home, engaging a realtor is not just beneficial; it is also essential. Their expertise, guidance, and unwavering support can make your home-buying journey not only smoother but also more rewarding.

But buying your first home is a big decision and a major investment, so you should do it with others. You should hire a buyer's agent who can help you find the best home for you and guide you through the process. A buyer's agent can save you time, money, and stress and make your home-buying experience enjoyable and successful.

So, don't hesitate to contact a buyer's agent today and start your journey to homeownership. Finding the perfect home-buying agent or REALTOR® is akin to discovering the ideal doctor, caretaker for your child, or financial advisor.

Therefore, you will need someone whom you can trust implicitly and someone who genuinely has your best interests at heart.

Before we move to the next chapter that deals with finding your ideal home, making an offer, and doing the necessary steps, you will need to consider the following tips when trying to find the homebuying agent who is the perfect match for your real estate dream.

Some Strategies to Remember
Signs of a Realtor Ally

1. **Client-Centric Approach:** Look for indicators of a client-first mentality. This includes testimonials emphasizing the realtor's ability to tailor their services to meet individual client needs.

2. **Listening Skills:** A realtor who actively listens and comprehends your vision demonstrates a commitment to finding the right fit, not just any property.

3. **Negotiation Prowess:** Inquire about their negotiation strategies. An adept negotiator can

secure the best terms and prices while safeguarding your interests.

Embracing Comfort in the Hunt

1. **Establish Priorities:** Prioritize your non-negotiables and must-haves. This helps narrow down options and eases decision-making.

2. **Pre-Approval:** Obtain a mortgage pre-approval. It not only streamlines the buying process but also strengthens your position in negotiations.

3. **Patience and Flexibility:** Be patient and flexible. The perfect home might appear slowly, but it's essential to remain adaptable to various possibilities.

Expand Your Search Horizons

1. **Online Platforms:** Explore reputable online platforms that feature realtor reviews and ratings. These resources offer insights into a realtor's professionalism, responsiveness, and dedication to client satisfaction.

2. **Industry Referrals:** Seek referrals not only from friends and family but also from industry professionals. Mortgage brokers, attorneys, or local housing authorities often have valuable recommendations based on their interactions with realtors.

3. **Local Presence:** Consider a realtor deeply entrenched in the local market. Their in-depth knowledge of neighborhoods, trends, and property histories can be invaluable in finding the ideal home.

Identifying Your Ideal Realtor

Selecting the right agent entails considering several critical aspects:

- **Experience:** Seek an agent with a proven track record of success.

- **Communication Style:** Ensure a comfortable and responsive communication dynamic.

- **Local Market Knowledge:** Prioritize an agent with an intimate understanding of the local market.

- **Negotiation Skills:** Assess their ability to negotiate effectively for your benefit.

The collaboration between a buyer and their realtors goes beyond a mere transaction. It's a partnership built on trust, expertise, and mutual respect, paving the way for a successful and fulfilling home-buying experience. Remember, your realtor isn't just a guide; they're your advocate in the pursuit of homeownership.

This chapter serves as a comprehensive guide, leveraging industry insights and professional perspectives to assist homebuyers in navigating the real estate landscape. By employing these strategies and leveraging professional advice, you'll pave the way to finding the perfect realtor and, ultimately, your dream home.

Chapter 7: We Like This One! What's Next?

Buying or selling a house is a major decision that involves many steps and details. One of the most important parts of the process is making or accepting an offer. This is where you negotiate the price and terms of the deal with the other party.

So, let us assume that you found the property that you would like to call your home. But you won't just go out there and make an offer. This is what a typical person, without professional help, might do, but it's wiser to let the experts take it from here. The reason for this is that transitioning from finding the right home to making an offer is one of the crucial steps that you are going to take.

The Process and Technicalities

Before we delve into the details, I would like you to understand the basic process of making an offer and clarify some of the terms that are used so you know the basics throughout the process.

1. **Determining the Offer Amount:** You will need to research the market value of similar properties in the area. Consider the home's condition, location, and recent sale prices. Your realtor or buying agent will help you in this step with a Comparative Market

Analysis (CMA). This will allow you to arrive at a reasonable offer amount.

2. **Preparation of Offer:** Your agent will then assist you in drafting an offer letter or contract, which will include the proposed purchase price, any contingencies such as home inspections, the desired timelines (closing date), and potential concessions such as those for repairs or seller-paid closing costs.

3. **Submitting the Offer:** Once you understand and are satisfied with the terms, your agent will then submit the offer to the seller's agent. Sellers may receive multiple offers, so your offer should be competitive yet realistic. Also, there should be space for an inclusion clause — so you may be able to outbid a higher bidder — but you should discuss this with your agent if it is required in your case or not since it's not always necessary.

4. **Negotiation:** Once an offer is made, it is up to the seller to accept, reject, or counter your offer. Negotiations are usually involved afterward. You may be involved in back-and-forth discussions until you and the seller reach an agreement on price and terms. You should be prepared for compromises and adjustments during this phase.

Please remember that the seller can also ignore an offer and does not have to counter. I have had sellers who totally ignore a low-ball offer and others who will counter with an offer above and beyond the original asking price because the low offer made them mad.

Remember also to put yourself in the other parties' shoes. Ask yourself if you would have accepted the offer if you were in the seller's place. Moreover, when negotiating, always leave your emotions out because you need to use facts to make up your mind.

5.   **Signing the Contract:** When both parties agree on the final terms, then you will finally be able to sign a purchase agreement or contract. This is a legally binding contract that ties you and the seller to the outlined terms, initiating the next steps in the home-buying process.

Most of the time, the buyer's agent will present a written offer to the seller's agent, who will then present it to the sellers. It is easier to start with a written offer, especially one that has many details in it, as these details may be added to or reduced as the contract goes back and forth between the agents representing the parties. That way, there is no way to forget any details as the deal goes back and forth in verbal negotiation.

A few terms that you will come across but you will need to be aware of are as follows:

- **Earnest Money:** This is the deposit money that shows your commitment to the purchase and is held in escrow. When the deal closes, the buyer is credited for the amount of earnest money against what is owed on the note. It is often between one and three percent of the deal, whereas some expensive properties and in-demand real-estate projects might require up to five percent as part of the earnest money.

If, for some reason, the deal does not close and there are vendors involved who have incurred expenses — for example, if plumbing repairs or a survey has been done then the earnest money will first go to satisfy any unpaid vendors. If there are no unpaid bills on the property, then both buyer and seller must agree on who will receive the earnest money, and they must sign a release in Texas. If they can't agree, then after two years, a judge will decide.

- **Contingencies:** As the word suggests, these are your backups against emergencies to protect you by allowing you to back out under specific conditions, such as inspections showing issues neither party will correct or financing issues. There are other contingencies, too.

For example, a buyer may have to sell his property before that buyer can buy this property. There may be a contingency that the property be eligible for an FHA, VA, or USDA loan. And many more depending on who is buying it and what purpose they intend to use it for.

- **Closing Date:** This is an agreed-upon timeline that suits you and the seller. It is decided after considering the time required for loan approval, inspections, adjustments, and moving arrangements. This date is not set in stone and can be changed if both parties agree.

For example, title companies may have the title work ready before the contract date, and the lender may also be ready to close. If the parties agree to move it up, then an amendment to the contract is prepared and signed. It can also be extended in the same manner.

- **Additional Terms:** This is your area to shine and for your agent to pick and choose what you like. For instance, if the seller needs to negotiate more on the price, then you may negotiate on additional conditions or requests, such as repairs or specific appliances or furnishings, to be included in the sale agreement.

It would be best if you remembered that each real estate transaction is unique, and so the process will vary slightly, too. You should always consult with your real estate agent or legal advisor for specific guidance which is best tailored to your situation.

According to the National Association of Realtors (NAR), analyzing the recent sale prices of comparable properties in the area — technically referred to as 'comparables' — can provide crucial insights into determining a competitive yet reasonable offer. While your realtor will do this for you, you can also do a bit of research on your own from famous platforms such as Zillow or Redfin to glance at some real-time data on comparable sales and market trends.

Once you have found a property that ticks all the right boxes for you and you're prepared to seal the deal, then it's time for you to strategize your offer. This process begins with a thorough analysis of the market as well as an evaluation of similar properties' sale prices in order to gauge the current demands.

To provide a true comparative market analysis, a realtor must use properties that are still on the market and properties that have sold recently. Most laypersons can not get the prices for properties already sold. In most cases, this information is not available except to real estate professionals. You can look at list prices all day long, but there will be little information regarding sold properties online.

A qualified realtor or buying agent will prove invaluable at this point of the journey since they have access to the data and market trends for neighborhoods.

Making an offer involves a delicate balance between presenting a competitive bid while staying within your budget.

Having access to this type of information will allow you to ascertain the right value for the property and estimate the additional work required on the home and its costs. This will mean that you spend your budget wisely, and you will also know how much extra money you can expect to keep bidding additionally or pay for other costs.

How to Make an Offer

The reason that I insist on finding the right professional for the job throughout the book will become clear when you want to approach a seller and make an offer. The expert plays a key role here, with whom you may either become lost or save a considerable amount of money in the home-buying process. Your trusted realtor or homebuyer's agent will consider a multitude of factors before they make an offer.

At the same time, they will conduct certain checks and keep an eye out for contingencies that will ensure your homebuying journey goes smoothly and effectively. The three key factors that are considered before making an offer are as follows:

- Home's condition.

- Market trends.

- The seller's motivation.

Most people might think of the first two factors before making an offer, but they fail to do so since they need to learn how the industry values the two things. The right professional knows these calculations and helps you understand them.

This is why communication with your buying agent or realtor is extremely important. Next, you should know that making an offer involves more than just knowing the right price tag or having enough money. As per the data from the profile of American homeowners from the National Association of Realtors (NAR), nearly two-thirds of successful homebuyers consider additional terms like flexible closing dates or including certain appliances or furniture.[6]

This flexibility could sway sellers in your favor, making your offer more appealing. Crafting a compelling offer, therefore, includes not only the price but also specific terms and contingencies — such as the proposed closing date and any additional requests on your behalf, such as offering to pay for repairs.

---

[6] National Association of Realtors, Highlights From the Profile of Home Buyers and Sellers, National Association of Realtors. November 13, 2023.
https://www.nar.realtor/research-and-statistics/research-reports/highlights-from-the-profile-of-home-buyers-and-sellers

Many first-time home buyers will want everything on the inspection report fixed. For example, in older homes, many electrical outlets will not be grounded, and the inspector will mention this in his report. It will be an expense in the thousands of dollars, and most sellers and buyers will not want the additional expense. This might be an issue that can be addressed later when the buyer has more funds.

But some issues must be addressed regardless, for example, the air conditioner or heater does not work. That must be addressed before closing by one party or the other, whatever they agree on. They could even split the expenses evenly.

The cost of an inspection varies, depending on the property's size and location. Your homebuying agent will help you in this regard and schedule it whenever you would like. It is wise to schedule this promptly after the offer's acceptance, too, since it will allow you enough time for potential renegotiations or contingencies in between — in case of additional or major issues. Remember, if there is an option period in the contract, it will start the day all parties have signed the contract. It is during this period that the inspection must be done, and any repairs needed must be listed in an amendment and sent to the seller's agent. If the seller is not willing to make the repairs, the buyer has the option to terminate the contract if it is within the option period.

Following the inspection, you should expect a comprehensive report that details the property's strengths and weaknesses. This report can serve as a negotiating tool, giving you the leverage to request repairs or adjustments to the sale price based on the significant findings. As per an article in Realtor Magazine by NAR, an inspection plays a critical role by providing an unbiased assessment of the property's condition.[7]

Having a thorough and professional inspection done will always keep you one step ahead of the way and allow you to plan well for your dream home. The paperwork involved at this stage includes the offer itself, the acceptance or counteroffer from the seller, and the agreement outlining inspection details and any subsequent negotiations.

Remember, this phase requires a prudent approach and sometimes swift decisions, so being prepared and having a real estate agent or lawyer to guide you through this stage can be immensely beneficial.

So, finally, all the guidance that I provided you with about being prepared for the mortgage process —

---

[7] Melissa Dittmann Tracey, Homeownership Horrors: What Can Go Wrong for Your Clients, Realtor Magazine. October 30, 2023.
https://www.nar.realtor/magazine/real-estate-news/sales-marketing/homeownership-horrors-what-can-go-wrong-for-your-clients

finding the right professionals and how to vet them — will fall into place in this part of your homebuying journey.

Here are some tips and guidelines to help you with this stage of your homebuying journey:

- **Your Home for Your Needs:** Before you make an offer, you should have a clear idea of how much you can afford and what kind of home you are looking for. This is why your loan's pre-approval process is important.

Your agent will help sort out the properties that match your criteria and show you the recent sales of similar homes in the area. It will help you determine the fair market value of the home and avoid overpaying or underbidding.

- **Submit An Offer:** If your dream home is in demand or a popular locality, then you may have to act fast to get the home you want. Your agent will help you prepare and submit an offer that includes the offer price, earnest money deposit, closing date, contingencies, and other terms.

You should also provide proof of your financial ability to buy the home, such as a pre-approval letter from your lender.

- **Be Ready to Negotiate:** The seller may accept, reject, or counter your offer. If the seller counters, you can either accept, reject, or counter back. The negotiation process may involve several rounds of offers and counteroffers until an agreement is reached. Your agent can advise you on how to negotiate effectively and strategically.

To be successful in your offer, you should consider some factors that can help you stand out from other buyers. These factors are as follows:

o **Write a Personal Letter**: Often, the seller has an emotional attachment to the home, which is why you can write a letter explaining why you would love to own the home and how you plan to take care of it. It can appeal to the seller's emotions and make your offer more memorable.

o **Using odd numbers:** Instead of rounding up or down to the nearest hundred or thousand, you can use odd numbers in your offer price. For instance, try offering $345,700 instead of $350,000. It can make your offer seem more precise and thoughtful, and it can also give you a slight edge over other buyers who will mostly offer round numbers.

Conclusion

By integrating the tips, insights, and data that I have provided to you so far, you will be able to have a well-rounded understanding of what it takes to transition from selecting a home to making an offer on it. Follow the advice contained in this chapter, and you will be able to make an offer that is well-appreciated by the home seller.

In the next chapter, I will explain what happens when an agreement is signed and what goes on behind during the processing stage.

Chapter 8: What Are the Lender and Title Company Doing After We Have Signed the Contract?

Now, you have found your dream home, made an offer, and got it accepted by the seller. In that case, congratulations! You are one step closer to becoming a homeowner. But before you can celebrate, you need to go through the closing process, which is the final and most crucial stage of the real estate transaction.

The closing process, which is also known as escrow, completion, or settlement, is when the ownership of the property is officially transferred from the seller to the buyer. It involves a lot of paperwork, coordination, and verification among various parties, such as the real estate agent, the lender, the title company, the attorney, and the escrow company.

There are a couple of things that I would like you to know that happen behind the stage once you have signed an agreement. The main stakeholders in this process are the lender, the title company, and your homebuying agent or realtor, who coordinate with one another and ensure that the possession process proceeds smoothly.

The Post-Contract Phase

The post-contract phase in real estate transactions involves intricate processes that are crucial for both buyers and sellers. This is why after the purchase agreement is signed, several behind-the-scenes processes kick in. At this stage, the lender plays a pivotal role — from collecting all the information, processing the mortgage application, conducting credit checks, and verifying financial details to assessing the property's value through an appraisal to determine loan eligibility. [8]

At the same time, the title company, which is responsible for transferring the property, steps in to ensure a clear title for the property. Their responsibility is to conduct a thorough title search to uncover any existing liens, encumbrances, or legal issues that might affect your ownership. This process involves examining public records to validate the seller's right to transfer ownership while ensuring that the buyer receives a clear and marketable title.

The title company is also responsible for the title insurance, which aims to safeguard the buyer against any unforeseen title defects or claims that might arise in the future. This insurance protects you or the buyer's investment and ensures peace of mind,

---

[8] A Step by Step Guide of What to Do Once You Have Signed a Purchase Agreement, Title Escrow Miami.

covering legal fees and potential losses associated with title disputes.

These behind-the-scenes processes are critical to the successful completion of a real estate transaction, ensuring the buyer receives a property with a clean title and securing the necessary financing for the purchase. Let me explain the importance of each step in depth before I can begin to describe the entire process in detail.

The mortgage application process involves comprehensive assessments. The Consumer Financial Protection Bureau (CFPB) plays an important role at this stage, where lenders meticulously review the buyer's credit history, income verification, employment details, and debt-to-income ratios. As per the research report published by the National Association of Realtors (NAR), nearly 88% of homebuyers finance their purchases through mortgages, which emphasizes the significance of lenders in the real estate market.[9]

Moreover, lenders also conduct property appraisals to determine its market value and ensure it aligns with the loan amount. The Federal Deposit

---

[9] National Association of Realtors, 2023 Profile of Homebuyers and sellers. nar.realtor. November 13, 2023. https://cdn.nar.realtor/sites/default/files/documents/2023-profile-of-home-buyers-and-sellers-highlights-11-13-2023.pdf

Insurance Corporation (FDIC) emphasizes the importance of this step to mitigate risks for both lenders and buyers. Meanwhile, the role of the title company in ensuring a clear title is fundamental.

In fact, research conducted by the American Land Title Association (ALTA) shows that title issues affect about a quarter of all real estate transactions.[10] ALTA's responsibility, hence, includes conducting a comprehensive title search that delves into public records, tax records, deeds, and other legal documents. This is the stage that helps identify any liens, encumbrances, or legal disputes that might cloud the title.

Furthermore, the findings from ALTA and NAR underscore the importance of title insurance. The Insurance Information Institute (III) also notes that title insurance protects buyers from potential legal claims or disputes, providing financial security and peace of mind. Some common title issues that can happen are: a missing heir must sign off on a previous transaction, the legal description of the property is incorrect and must be corrected, and tax or city liens must be paid before the property can change owners.

---

[10] Joe, Jentile, California Land Title Association,
Title Insurance Protects Your Biggest Investment for not a Lot of Cost, Washington Post. April 8, 2015. https://www.clta.org/page/article3

Almost all real estate experts indicate that a clear title is non-negotiable in most real estate transactions. A clouded title can lead to delays, additional costs, or even the cancellation of the transaction. This underlines the critical role of the title company in ensuring a smooth transfer of ownership.

The data and insights provided so far underscore the significance of the behind-the-scenes processes post-contract in real estate transactions, which emphasizes the pivotal roles of both lenders and title companies in securing a successful property purchase. If you are ready to buy a home and want to finalize everything, then this chapter is for you!

The Closing Process

The final closing process can take anywhere from a few days to a few months, depending on the complexity of the deal, the type of financing, and the preferences of the buyer and seller. To ensure a smooth and successful closing, you need to understand what happens behind the scenes, what your role and responsibilities are, and what potential issues or delays you may encounter.

This is why I explained the importance of this process and what roles the lender and mortgage expert play. Now, let me get into the details of what happens after the purchase agreement has been finalized and the closing process has started. In doing so, I will also provide some tips and best practices to help you prepare for and navigate the closing process with confidence and ease.

Given that this stage of home-buying is the most technical and time-consuming, I would like to sum it up in ten steps so that you may clearly understand and come back to it whenever you are in the post-contract phase.

Summing Up the Ten-Step Process

Given that the purchase agreement is the contract that outlines the terms and conditions of the sale, such as the price, the contingencies, the closing date, and the responsibilities of each party. The closing process begins once both the buyer and the seller sign the contract. It is a rather long process, but I will divide it into ten easy-to-understand steps that should provide you with an overview of the process.

The first step is to open an escrow account, which is a secure and neutral account that is held by a third party — usually an escrow company or a title company. The escrow account serves as a safe place to deposit the earnest money, the down payment, the closing costs, and the documents related to the sale. Therefore, the escrow agent acts as a mediator between the buyer and the seller and ensures that all the contractual obligations are met before releasing the funds and the documents.

As described earlier, the second step is to perform a title search and purchase a title insurance policy. The title search is, thus, a process of verifying the legal ownership and the ownership history of the property. It involves checking the public records for any liens, judgments, easements, encumbrances, or defects that may affect the title.

A title insurance policy offers protection against any claims or losses that may arise from a title defect or dispute. The title company or the attorney will conduct the title search and issue the title insurance policy, which the lender usually requires, and the buyer.

The third step is to hire a closing attorney if needed. A closing attorney is a legal expert who can review the closing documents, explain the legal terms and implications, and represent your interests in case of any disputes or problems. Depending on the state and the complexity of the transaction, hiring a closing attorney may either be optional or mandatory.

Even if it is not required, it is advisable to consult with a closing attorney before you close a deal to ensure that you understand and agree with everything you are signing.

The fourth step is to get pre-approved for a mortgage if you still need to do so. A mortgage pre-approval is a letter from a lender that states how much money you can borrow, what interest rate you qualify for, and what your monthly payments will be. As explained in the chapter before, the mortgage's pre-approval is not a guarantee of a loan, but it shows the seller that you are a serious and qualified buyer who can secure the financing in time for the closing. It also helps you set a realistic budget and narrow down your home search.

The fifth step is to determine your closing costs and how to pay for them. Closing costs are the fees and expenses that you need to pay at the closing, such as the appraisal fee, the inspection fee, the origination fee, the title insurance fee, the attorney fee, the recording fee, the prorated property tax, and the escrow fee.

Closing costs vary depending on the location, the type of property, the type of loan, and the lender, but they typically range from 2% to 5% of the purchase price. You can either pay the closing costs out of pocket or negotiate with the seller or the lender to cover some or all of them.

The sixth step is to complete the home inspection and the appraisal. A home inspection is a visual examination of the physical condition and the systems of the property, such as the roof, the foundation, the plumbing, the electrical system, the heating, and the cooling system. It is usually performed by a licensed and certified home inspector who will provide a detailed report of the findings and recommendations.

While a home inspection is not mandatory, it is highly recommended, as it can reveal any hidden issues or defects that may affect the value or the safety of the property. A home inspection can also give you the opportunity to request repairs or credits from the seller or to back out of the deal if the issues are too severe. An appraisal is an estimate of the market value of the property based on the recent sales of comparable properties in the area, the features and the condition of the property, and the current market trends.

It is usually done by a licensed and certified appraiser, who will provide a written report of the valuation and the methodology. The lender requires an appraisal, as it determines how much money they are willing to lend you. Suppose the appraisal comes in lower than the purchase price. In that case, you may have to renegotiate the price with the seller, make up the difference with a larger down payment, or find another lender or another property.

The seventh step is to finalize the mortgage application and the loan terms. Once you have the purchase agreement, the title report, the inspection report, and the appraisal report, then you can go on to submit your mortgage application to the lender — along with the required documents, such as your income statements, your bank statements, your tax returns, and your credit reports. The lender will then process your application and verify your information, which may take anywhere between a few days to a few weeks.

The lender will also conduct a final credit check and a final employment verification before approving your loan. Once your loan is approved, the lender will send you a loan estimate, which is a document that summarizes the key terms and costs of your loan, such as the interest rate, the monthly payment, the closing costs, and the annual percentage rate (APR).

You should review the loan estimate carefully and compare it with other offers, if any. It would be best if you also asked the lender any questions or clarifications that you may have. If you are satisfied with the loan estimate, you can lock in the interest rate and the loan terms with the lender, which means that they will not change until the closing unless there are any significant changes in your situation or the market.

The eighth step is to review the closing disclosure and the closing documents. The closing disclosure is a document that provides the final and actual terms and costs of your loan, such as the interest rate, the monthly payment, the closing costs, and the APR. The closing disclosure is sent by the lender at least three business days before the closing, and it may differ from the loan estimate, depending on the changes in the loan terms or the closing costs.

You should compare the closing disclosure with the loan estimate and check for any errors or discrepancies. It would be best if you also asked the lender any questions or clarifications that you may have. The closing documents are the legal papers that you need to sign at the closing, such as the promissory note, the deed of trust, the affidavit of title, the transfer tax declaration, and the settlement statement.

The closing documents are prepared by the closing attorney or the title company, and they are sent to you for review at least one day before the closing. You should read the closing documents carefully and understand what you are signing. You should also ask the closing attorney or the title company any questions or clarifications that you may have.

The ninth step is to conduct a final walk-through of the property. A final walk-through is a last inspection of the property before the closing wrap-up, which is usually done within 24 hours of the closing. The purpose of the final walk-through is to make sure that the property is in the same or better condition as when you made the offer — that the seller has completed any agreed-upon repairs or improvements, and that the seller has removed all their personal belongings and trash and that the seller has left behind any items that were included in the sale, such as appliances, fixtures, or furniture.

You should bring a copy of the purchase agreement or contract, the inspection report, and the repair receipts to the final walk-through, and you should check every room, closet, cabinet, and drawer. You should also test the appliances, the faucets, the toilets, the lights, the outlets, the doors, the windows, and the locks. If you find any issues or damage, you should take photos and videos, and you should notify your agent and the seller immediately.

You should also request a remedy or compensation from the seller, or you should delay the closing until the issues are resolved. The tenth step is to attend the closing meeting and sign the closing documents. The closing meeting is the final and official meeting where the ownership of the property is transferred from the seller to the buyer.

The closing meeting is usually held at the office of the escrow company, the title company, or the closing attorney, and it may take a few hours. The buyer and the seller attend the closing meeting, as well as the buyer's agent, the seller's agent, the lender's representative, the escrow agent, the title agent, and the closing attorney. At this meeting, you will need to bring the following items:

- A government-issued photo ID, such as a driver

- Your legal documents, including the lending and pre-mortgage documents.

In this chapter, we covered what happens behind the scenes once an agreement is signed and who the important stakeholders are in this part of the homebuying journey.

It is important to know the process, duties, and responsibilities so that you can not only know what to expect in the process but also accept how long the approval takes. Being prepared and informed of these crucial aspects will ensure that your agreement is accepted and the closing meeting goes smoothly. The information provided in this chapter will prove itself crucial when you either have to or want to make changes to the contract.

In the next chapter, we will discuss what to do when amendments have to be made in a contract, what possible reasons cause such changes, and how the negotiation process unfolds in this part of your home-buying process.

Chapter 9: Gahh! We Have to Change the Contract!

Following the post-contract phase, you must have eagerly waited for weeks to move into your dream home. So what happens next? Your agent congratulates you because you have found your dream home, navigated the offer frenzy, and finally secured that coveted execution date on your contract.

While this all appears quite dreamy, you should hold your horses at this point and take a step back. Often, changes have to be made in the contract. In this chapter, I will explain why amendments may have to be made and how you can navigate them effectively to ensure that you have the right contract for your dream home.

But hold on, intrepid adventurer, because the journey doesn't end there.

Whatever Happens, Happens for a Reason

Usually, while the ink on the contract paper may appear dry, life might throw curveballs that necessitate amending your meticulously crafted contract.

In such a case, there is no need to panic or fear. This chapter will equip you with the tools to navigate and succeed through this final process of technicalities and bureaucracy. So, to understand this part, imagine your contract as a blueprint that scrupulously outlines the terms of your homeownership adventure.

However, just like blueprints in any grand construction project, unforeseen circumstances might arise, which necessitate making adjustments. Upon closer inspection of the deal, you will find the hidden crevices, such as when the appraisal falls short, or your life takes an unexpected turn that requires you to change the closing date.

These are just a few examples where contract amendments become your compass, guiding you toward a mutually agreeable solution. So, how do you navigate this contract-altering terrain with confidence and grace?

Here is your roadmap and some things that you need to be on the lookout for:

Identifying the Need for Change

The first step is recognizing the need for an amendment. You should clearly avoid panicking, especially not at the slightest hiccups. Please note that minor issues can arise and are often easily addressed by your agent and title company.

There is a reason why things are not rushed: no one wants you to suffer or be wronged in the long run. Similarly, you also want flexibility on where you work according to your requirements. This is why there is an expansive framework that exists around the world of contracts.

However, significant discrepancies such as unforeseen structural damage or inaccurate property valuations might warrant an amendment. So, what are the common scenarios that might lead to amendments?

The following are some situations where contract amendments might come into play:

Sale Price Negotiation

Unexpected repairs might necessitate a renegotiation of the price. Approach this with data and a clear understanding of the market value. Have a look at the following example of what can happen before the night of closing:

Imagine if, before the night of the closing, there was a storm that damaged the roof of your soon-to-be home. The seller may ask that you share the cost of those repairs in an amendment or simply reduce the price of the house by the repairs.

Whatever both parties agree can be added to an amendment to the contract. Such unexpected changes can occur, so we have to be prepared for untoward situations.

Inclusion of Additional Items

Did the seller forget to mention that the gorgeous chandelier is reserved, but you can have it for another small increase in the price of the property? You can negotiate its inclusion in the deal through an amendment.

Closing Date Adjustment

Job relocation, unforeseen personal circumstances, or financing delays might require a change in the closing date. Open communication with the seller is key here.

Inspection Reveals Hidden Issues

Minor structural problems, pest infestations, or faulty appliances might require repair or price concessions. An amendment is the way to handle these situations.

Understand that a contract amendment is a written document that modifies or adds to the original terms and conditions of a contract. They are needed when there are changes in the circumstances or expectations of either party that affect the contract. Moreover, they are signed by both parties and attached to the original contract as part of the legal record.

For example, you may discover some defects or damages in the property during the inspection or appraisal process. You may want to negotiate a lower sale price or ask the seller to fix them before closing. You could also include some additional items in the deal, such as appliances, furniture, or fixtures, that were not part of the original contract.

Or you may encounter some delays or difficulties in securing your financing or meeting other contingencies and need to extend the closing date or cancel the contract altogether.

Negotiating with Confidence

Remember, contract amendments are a collaborative effort. Here is how to approach them effectively:

Open Communication

Maintain transparency with the seller and your agent. Explain your concerns clearly and provide supporting documentation, which may include inspection reports, appraisals, etc.

Focus on Solutions

Do not dwell on blame. Instead, propose creative solutions that benefit and bridge the gap between both parties, like price adjustments or repair credits.

Seek Professional Guidance

Consult your agent and lawyer to understand the legal implications of any amendments. Their expertise can ensure a smooth and fair process.

Know Your Limits

While compromise is vital, do not compromise your core needs or financial stability. Be prepared to walk away if the agreement does not align with your priorities.

Making Changes in Contract

Negotiating contract changes can be a challenging and stressful process, especially if you are emotionally attached to the property or under time pressure. However, it is important to remember that contract changes are not uncommon, and they can be resolved amicably and fairly with the help of your real estate agent and lawyer.

Here are some tips on how to negotiate contract changes:

Communicate clearly and promptly: As soon as you encounter a situation that requires a contract change, inform your real estate agent and lawyer and explain your reasons and expectations. They will communicate with the seller's agent and lawyer and try to find a mutually acceptable solution. Do not wait until the last minute or try to handle the situation yourself, as this may create misunderstandings or conflicts.

Be flexible and realistic: Understand that contract changes are a two-way street, and you may need to compromise or make some concessions to reach an agreement. For example, if you want to lower the sale price because of some defects in the property, you may have to accept some minor issues that are not worth fixing or pay for some of the repairs yourself. Or, if you want to include some additional items in the deal, you may have to pay extra or give up some other items that were originally included. Or, if you need to extend the closing date, you may have to pay some additional earnest money to the seller for the delay.

Be respectful and courteous: Remember that the seller is also a human being who may have their own emotions and expectations about the property and the contract. Do not make unreasonable or insulting demands or accusations that may offend or antagonize the seller. Instead, try to understand their perspective and show empathy and appreciation for their cooperation. A positive and respectful attitude can go a long way in building trust and rapport and facilitating a smooth and successful transaction.

What are the implications of contract changes?

Contract changes can have various implications for both parties, depending on the nature and extent of the changes. Some of the possible implications are as follows:

Legal Implications

Contract changes may affect the legal rights and obligations of both parties, such as the transfer of title, the payment of taxes and fees, the liability for damages or defects, and the recourse for breach or default. Therefore, it is essential to consult your lawyer before agreeing to any contract changes and to ensure that the changes are properly documented and executed in accordance with the law.

Financial Implications

Contract changes may affect the financial aspects of the transaction, such as the sale price, the closing costs, and the financing terms. Therefore, it is important to consult your lender before agreeing to any contract changes involving financing to ensure that you have sufficient funds and credit to complete the transaction.

Emotional Implications

Contract changes may affect the emotional state of both parties, such as their satisfaction, confidence, and attachment to the property. Therefore, it is advisable to consult your family before agreeing to any contract changes and to ensure that you are comfortable and happy with the outcome.

Conclusion

Making changes in the contract is a common part of the home-buying process. However, it does not have to be a daunting or unpleasant experience. In the next and final chapter, we will discuss the closing process and how to prepare for it. So stay tuned!

Chapter 10: Finally, the Day of Closing is Almost Here!

You are nearing the pinnacle of your home-buying journey— the closing day. This moment marks the culmination of weeks or months of searching, negotiations, inspections, and paperwork. As you take your final steps, it is essential to stay organized and prepared for the big day.

At this stage, butterflies flutter in your stomach, a giddy mix of excitement and apprehension. The countdown to closing day is on, and your dream house awaits you with open arms and freshly painted doors, hopefully! But before you bask in the glory of homeownership, there are a few remaining hurdles that I would like you to know about.

Let us navigate them together and ensure a smooth, celebratory closing experience. There are a handful of things that homeowners should ideally keep in mind when moving in and finalizing the documentation. I have compiled a list of things that you should remember when you reach this stage so that nothing important is missed.

Your Final Checklist for the Big Day

There are four main parts of the checklist for the final day. You need to be mainly concerned with going through some of the things a day or two earlier, then a few basic things (including mental exercises) that are to be done on the closing day. Finally, a couple of paperwork tips and an overview will allow you to get through everything in an organized and professional manner.

1. Final Walkthrough

- Schedule a final walkthrough with the seller 24-48 hours before closing day. It is your chance to confirm if everything is in order as per the contract.

- Check for repairs, renovations, and appliances mentioned in the agreement.

- Arrive on time for the closing appointment. Delays can cause complications, so ensure you have allotted sufficient time for the process.

- Sometimes, unexpected issues might arise during the closing. Stay flexible and patient to address any last-minute hiccups calmly.

- Inspect for any new damage or discrepancies since your last visit.

- Do not be shy about voicing concerns; remember, you have the right to renegotiate or postpone closing if necessary.

2. Paperwork Prowess

• Collect all the essential documents required for closing. The requested documents can include the following: loan documents, homeowner's insurance proof, your ID, and any other closing-related paperwork.

• Review, understand, and clarify any doubts with your lender or closing agent before giving the final go-ahead.

• Sign and return documents promptly to avoid any untoward delays.

3. Financial Fitness

• Ensure that your closing funds are readily available in the designated account.

• Consider setting aside some buffer money for unforeseen expenses that you might have to do upon moving — such as basic furniture, equipment, improvements, etc.

What to Expect on the Closing Day

The venue for the closing day might be a boring office or an elegant and charming title company, but the atmosphere should be electric with your anticipation of closing the deal for good!

The following are some of the things that I would like you to consider before you go. These will allow you to understand what to expect when you are there.

Do Not Hesitate to Ask Questions

Communicate openly with your lender, realtor, and closing agent to avoid misunderstandings and delays. No question is too small when it comes to your finances and home. Seek clarification on any fees or terms you do not understand.

Be Prepared For Minor Hiccups

Closing delays can happen due to paperwork errors or unforeseen issues. Stay calm and flexible, and work with your team to find solutions.

Sign Once You Have Reviewed

The closing agent will meticulously guide you through the final documents, explaining each term and answering any questions. Take time to carefully review the '*Closing Disclosure*' provided by your lender. Verify that all the details, including loan terms, closing costs, and any credits or adjustments, align with your expectations and previous discussions.

You should sign only when you are satisfied with everything! Consider this your chance to spot errors and save yourself some time and money in advance. So inspect and read closely, keep an open mind, and calm yourself down!

Funding and Title Transfer

Coordinate with your bank or financial institution to ensure that the necessary funds for closing, including the down payment and closing costs, are ready and available in the appropriate account. Your lender will then transfer the mortgage funds to the seller's account, officially making you the proud owner of your dream house!

A recent study by the National Association of Realtors (NAR) has revealed that the average closing costs for first-time homebuyers in the US are, on average, under 3.7% percent of the loan amount.[11] While it can be a hefty sum to bear or arrange in advance

---

[11] Melissa Dittmann Tracey, States Where Closing Costs Are Highest, Lowest. National Association of Realtors. November 3, 2023.
https://www.nar.realtor/magazine/real-estate-news/states-where-closing-costs-are-highest-lowest

The Curtain is Unveiled

The moment you have been waiting for is finally here! You will receive the keys to your new home, marking the start of a beautiful chapter of your life. With the closing formalities complete, a wave of relief and exhilaration will wash over you.

'*You did it!*' should be the one thing that you should keep in mind at this stage. You struggled and reached this far to go through the homebuying process. You are officially a homeowner now!

The closing day marks the end of your home-buying journey and the start of a new chapter in your life. By staying organized, informed, and proactive, you can ensure a smooth and successful first home purchase.

Remember, this is an exciting milestone—celebrate it and enjoy the thrill of finally owning your dream home!